American Graphic Design Awards

No. 2

Visual Reference Publications/New York

Copyright © 2002 by Kaye Publishing Corp.

Visual Reference Publications, Inc.
302 Fifth Avenue
New York, NY 10001

Distributors to the trade in the United States and Canada
Watson-Guptill
770 Broadway
New York, NY 10003

Distributors outside the United States and Canada
HarperCollins International
10 East 53rd Street
New York, NY 10022

Library of Congress Cataloging in Publication Data:
American Graphic Design Awards No. 2
Printed in Hong Kong
ISBN 1-58471-066-7

CONTENTS

WELCOME TO THE DESIGN ANNUAL

For the twenty-first year, we offer for your viewing pleasure a select handful of the nearly 11,000 pieces entered in our American Graphic Design Awards program. The pieces that follow represent the best of American graphic design and business communications across the remarkably wide range of clients, projects and media that creative professionals touch.

Print and point-of-purchase, publications and packaging, invitations and collateral, internet and broadcast design, it's all there in a show of just how important graphic design is — and, in particular, the winners are — in shaping the look and feel of commerce and culture.

The showcased pieces represent something of transcendent value. In light of the horrific events of Sept. 2001, they are a visual manifestation of an American society and culture that is creative and free, democratic and diverse, entrepreneurial and energetic, imperfect but evolving.

Exactly the opposite of the repressive, brittle, inward, hate-filled misogynistic world that the terrorists — their state sponsors and apologists — would foist upon us.

Great designers grow and dream and create. This book humbly commemorates their contribution and, in so doing, contrasts nicely with how Osama bin Laden and his ilk will be remembered. As suggested by Tom Friedman of *The New York Times*, bin Laden's epitaph will likely read thus: "He destroyed much, he built nothing. His lasting impact was like a footprint in the desert."

GORDON KAYE   Publisher
LAURA ROTH   Director, American Graphic Design Awards
JAN SCHORR   Associate Director, American Grahic Design Awards
ILANA GREENBERG   Art Director
SUSAN BENSON   Editor
RACHEL GOLDBERG   Production Manager

RICK BONELLI

SUSAN CONSALES

JARED EBERHARDT

DOUGLAS GILBEY

JUDGES

6.

RICK BONELLI

Principal/Creative Director
Sunspots Creative, Inc., Hoboken NJ

Rick Bonelli founded Sunspots Creative with his wife and business partner, Deena Hartley, in 1996. The company specializes in concept-driven design in the areas of advertising, 3-D sales promotion, identity graphics, packaging and multimedia. His work has been featured in numerous national advertising and graphic design publications for a versatile client list including Accudart, Sharp, Avery Boardman, Lucent and Nielsen & Bainbridge. Bonelli is also a past Best of Show winner from the Art Directors Club of New Jersey; he received Best of Advertising honors at the 2000 Jersey Awards. He currently sits on the Board of Directors for the Advertising Club of New Jersey.

SUSAN CONSALES

Senior Vice President/Design Director
Sheppard Associates, Glendale CA

As senior vice president and design director with Sheppard Associates, Susan Consales uses design as a strategic tool for providing clients with effective solutions to their communication needs. She draws upon her 16 years of design and design management experience to understand the client's perspective and business goals, as well as the designer's perspective and creative approach to meeting those goals. Clients include MetLife, BellSouth, 3M, BP Amoco and Eastman Kodak. Consales holds a bachelor's degree in graphic design from the Rhode Island School of Design and a bachelor's degree in design from the University of California, Los Angeles.

JARED EBERHARDT

Brand Manager, Four Star Distribution
Salt Lake City UT

As brand manager for Four Star Distribution, a San Clemente-based company which owns, markets and distributes four of the snowboard and skateboard industry's leading brands (Special Blend Outerwear, Forum Snowboards, Foursquare Outerwear, and CircaFootwear), Eberhardt is responsible for creating and maintaining the image of a product line from inception to production. He integrates his philosophy of branding and the snow/skate culture into the marketing and the design of a softgoods and hardgoods line. Prior to joining Four Star Distribution, Eberhardt was a design director at Jager DiPaola Kemp. While at JDK he worked primarily on the Burton Snowboards account and directed a team of seven designers to create an onslaught of Burton Snowboards' marketing materials, including tv commercials, catalogs and advertisements.

DOUGLAS GILBEY

Inhouse Art Director/Project Manager
Amerock Corporation, Rockford IL

Douglas Gilbey is responsible for creative and strategic design of projects related to print, packaging, electronic media, and point-of-purchase displays for the retail and industrial market. As inhouse art director/project manager for Amerock, a division of Newell Rubbermaid cabinet hardware manufacturer, his daily responsibilities include project management, vendor coordination, account management and customer service. Gilbey has over nine years of previous design and print production experience with a BFA in visual communications and design from Northern Illinois University.

MARY LESTER

Executive Director, Art & Design
CXO Media, Framingham MA

Mary Lester is behind the classic design of CXO Media's two publications, CIO and Darwin. A seasoned designer, she joined the firm nearly 14 years ago when CIO magazine was publishing its fourth issue. Throughout Lester's tenure, she has maintained CIO's classic look and feel while keeping current with the changing demands of its readers. In the fall of 1999, Lester teamed up with editor in chief Abbie Lundberg to lead CIO through a complete redesign, including increased page size, perfect binding, bolder typography and more illustration, photography and white space. In June 2000, CXO Media launched Darwin magazine, creating a new challenge for the design team. Lester now manages a staff of 15 and oversees the management and artistic direction of both CIO (published 23 times per year) and Darwin (published monthly). Prior to CXO Media, Lester was a designer for Gill Fishman Associates and design group manager for Harvard University publications. She holds a BFA in visual communications from Northern Illinois University. Lester admits to a longstanding fascination with magazines since childhood and is "embarrassed to admit how many magazines come into her home monthly."

MARY LESTER

MIKE QUON

President/Creative Director
Designation Inc., New York NY

A Los Angeles native and graduate of the UCLA School of Design, Mike Quon came to New York City 25 years ago to meet the design world head on. He's been at it ever since, creating memorable graphic communications, corporate identity programs, advertising campaigns, exhibition design, and illustration for leading corporations, ad agencies, and non-profit organizations. As president and creative director of his Soho-based design firm, Designation Inc., Quon produces a wide range of projects, including recent logo identities for Pfizer and Aveda/ Estee Lauder, and campaigns for KPMG, Gateway Computer and Verizon. Mike Quon art has been seen around the world, from department stores in Tokyo and Paris, to events like World Cup Soccer and last year's Summer Olympics in Australia. A new Quon logo will even be making an appearance in an upcoming film by Woody Allen. Author of two books, "Non-Traditional Design" and "Corporate Graphics," Quon is able to take his design into many realms. "No matter what we're working on, it's always about communication," says Quon. "You have to understand the client's message and find the best visual way to make it sing."

MIKE QUON

DIANE STERMAN

Creative Director
Marriott.com, Bethesda MD

Diane Sterman is creative director for Marriott International's online portal, Marriott.com. She birthed Marriott's inhouse interactive design group five years ago while heading up design for Marriott's Creative Services group. Sterman comments: "I have the unique opportunity to work with the corporate internal design, marketing and information systems disciplines, as well as external cream of the crop agencies and individuals."

DIANE STERMAN

1

2

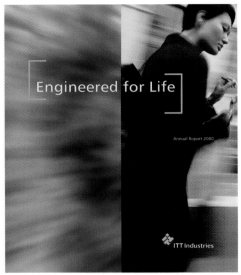

3

4

5

1 **DESIGN FIRM** Addison, New York, NY
CLIENT International Flavors & Fragrances
PROJECT 2000 Annual Report
ART DIRECTOR David Kohler
DESIGNER David Phan

2 **DESIGN FIRM** Addison, New York, NY
CLIENT The McGraw-Hill Companies
PROJECT 2000 Annual Report
ART DIRECTOR David Kohler
DESIGNER Nicolas Zentner

3 **DESIGN FIRM** Addison, New York, NY
CLIENT ITT Industries
PROJECT 2000 Annual Report
ART DIRECTOR Paul Sternglass
DESIGNER Paul Sternglass
PHOTOGRAPHER Jim Sims
ILLUSTRATOR James Noel Smith

4 **DESIGN FIRM** Addison, New York, NY
CLIENT Diebold, Incorporated
PROJECT 2000 Annual Report
ART DIRECTOR Richard Colbourne
DESIGNER John Moon
PHOTOGRAPHER Keith Ng

5 **DESIGN FIRM** Addison, New York, NY
CLIENT Engelhard Corporation
PROJECT 2000 Annual Report
ART DIRECTOR David Kohler
DESIGNER Chris Yun
PHOTOGRAPHER Brad Trent

1

2

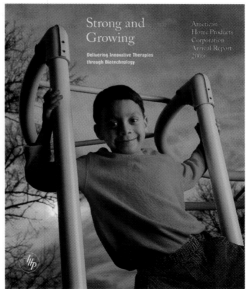

3

4

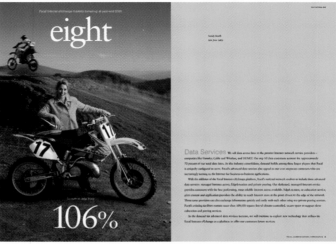

5

1 **DESIGN FIRM** Addison, New York, NY
CLIENT Bowne & Co., Inc.
PROJECT 2000 Annual Report
ART DIRECTOR David Kohler
DESIGNER Chris Yun
PHOTOGRAPHER David Katzenstein

2 **DESIGN FIRM** Arnold Saks Associates,
New York, NY
CLIENT SG Cowen Securities Corporation
PROJECT Uncommon Insight
ART DIRECTOR Arnold Saks
DESIGNER Robert Yasharian

3 **DESIGN FIRM** Arnold Saks Associates,
New York, NY
CLIENT American Home Products
PROJECT Strong and Growing
ART DIRECTOR Arnold Saks
DESIGNER Robert Yasharian

4 **DESIGN FIRM** Boller Coates & Neu, Chicago, IL
CLIENT Sara Lee Corporation
PROJECT 2000 Annual Report
ART DIRECTOR Ron Coates
DESIGNER Carolin Coates
PHOTOGRAPHERS Sandro Miller,
Andy Goodwin

5 **DESIGN FIRM** Boller Coates & Neu, Chicago, IL
CLIENT Focal Communications Corp.
PROJECT 2000 Annual Report
ART DIRECTOR Carolin Coates
DESIGNER Carolin Coates
PHOTOGRAPHER James Schnepf

1

2

3

4

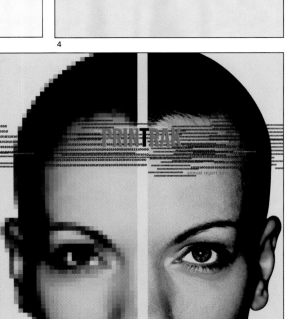

5

1 **DESIGN FIRM** Boller Coates & Neu, Chicago, IL
CLIENT Motorola, Inc.
PROJECT 2000 Summary Annual Report
ART DIRECTOR Ron Coates
DESIGNER Carolin Coates
PHOTOGRAPHERS Sandro Miller, Andy Goodwin

2 **DESIGN FIRM** Boller Coates & Neu, Chicago, IL
CLIENT Adolph Coors Company
PROJECT Annual Report 2000
ART DIRECTOR Ron Coates
DESIGNER Carolin Coates
PHOTOGRAPHER James Schnepf

3 **DESIGN FIRM** Boller Coates & Neu, Chicago, IL
CLIENT General Motors Corporation
PROJECT Annual Report 2000
ART DIRECTOR Harri Boller
DESIGNER James Pitroski
PHOTOGRAPHER Sandro Miller

4 **DESIGN FIRM** Carla Hall Design Group,
New York, NY
CLIENT Memorial Sloan-Kettering Cancer Center
PROJECT 2000 Annual Report
ART DIRECTORS Michael Wiemeyer, Carla Hall
DESIGNER John Stislow
PHOTOGRAPHER Robert Lisak

5 **DESIGN FIRM** CMg Design Inc., Pasadena, CA
CLIENT Printrak International, Inc.
PROJECT Annual Report 2000
ART DIRECTORS Greg Crawford, Julie Markfield
DESIGNER Jean DeAngelis

1

2

3

4

5

1 **DESIGN FIRM** CMg Design Inc., Pasadena, CA
CLIENT Rainbow Technologies Inc.
PROJECT Annual Report 2000
ART DIRECTORS Greg Crawford, Julie Markfield
DESIGNER Donna Pilcher-Gedeon
PHOTOGRAPHER Rick Ueda
ILLUSTRATOR Donna Pilcher-Gedeon

2 **DESIGN FIRM** Critt Graham & Associates, Atlanta, GA
CLIENT Knight Trading Group Inc.
PROJECT The Power of Options
DESIGNERS Kimie Ishii, Randy Allison
PHOTOGRAPHER George Lange

3 **DESIGN FIRM** Davidoff Associates Inc., New York, NY
CLIENT The Pepsi Bottling Group, Inc.
PROJECT Annual Report 2000
ART DIRECTORS Roger Davidoff, Patrina Marino
DESIGNERS Roger Davidoff, Patrina Marino
PHOTOGRAPHER Steve Fenn

4 **DESIGN FIRM** DeForest Creative Group, Ltd., Elmhurst, IL
CLIENT TTX Company
PROJECT 2000 Annual Report
ART DIRECTOR Wendy Weaver
DESIGNER Wendy Weaver
ILLUSTRATOR Wendy Weaver

5 **DESIGN FIRM** Dennis Johnson Design, Oakland, CA
CLIENT Rosenberg Foundation
PROJECT Report 1994-1999
ART DIRECTORS Dennis Johnson, Bill Goidell, Shelley Eades
DESIGNER Dennis Johnson
PHOTOGRAPHERS Robert Gumpert, Ken Light

1

2

3

4

5

1 **DESIGN FIRM** Directions Incorporated, Neenah, WI
CLIENT Fox Valley Technical College Foundation
PROJECT 1999-2000 Annual Report
ART DIRECTOR Chris Schudy
CREATIVE DIRECTOR Lori Daun
DESIGNER Ann Patras
PHOTOGRAPHER Munroe Studios
COPYWRITER Emily Anderson

2 **DESIGN FIRM** Douglas Joseph Partners,
Los Angeles, CA
CLIENT California Water Service Group
PROJECT 2000 Annual Report
ART DIRECTORS Douglas Joseph, Scott Lambert
DESIGNER Mark Schwartz
PHOTOGRAPHER Chris Shinn

3 **DESIGN FIRM** Edge Communications, Inc.,
Hermosa Beach, CA
CLIENT Norris Foundation
PROJECT 2000 Annual Report
ART DIRECTOR Phil Sato
DESIGNER Judy Woo
PHOTOGRAPHER Patrick Knisley

4 **DESIGN FIRM** Emerson, Wajdowicz Studios,
New York, NY
CLIENT Girl Scouts of the USA
PROJECT 2000 Annual Report
ART DIRECTOR Lisa LaRochelle
DESIGNERS Lisa LaRochelle, Jurek Wajdowicz
PHOTOGRAPHER Lori Adamski-Peek

5 **DESIGN FIRM** Emerson, Wajdowicz Studios,
New York, NY
CLIENT The Rockefeller Foundation
PROJECT 2000 Annual Report
ART DIRECTOR Jurek Wajdowicz
DESIGNERS Lisa LaRochelle, Jurek Wajdowicz,
Yoko Yoshida
PHOTOGRAPHER Antonin Kratochvil

1

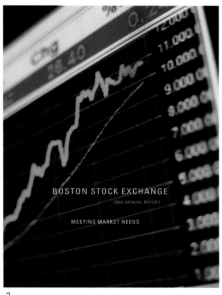

2

3

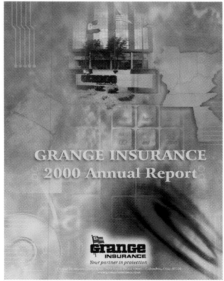

4

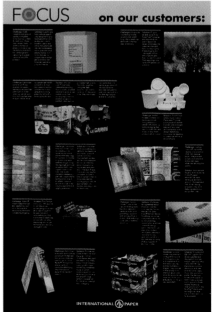

5

1 **DESIGN FIRM** Firefly Design & Communications Inc., New York, NY
CLIENT Medical Liability Mutual Insurance Company
PROJECT 2000 Annual Report
ART DIRECTOR Sheila Cobb
DESIGNER Heather Sears

2 **DESIGN FIRM** Gill Fishman Associates, Cambridge, MA
CLIENT Boston Stock Exchange
PROJECT 2000 Annual Report
ART DIRECTOR Gill Fishman
DESIGNER Dori Smith
PHOTOGRAPHER George Simian

3 **DESIGN FIRM** Gill Fishman Associates, Cambridge, MA
CLIENT Precise Software Solutions
PROJECT 2000 Annual Report
ART DIRECTOR Gill Fishman
DESIGNER Alicia Ozyjowski

4 **DESIGN FIRM** Grange Insurance, Columbus, OH
PROJECT 2000 Annual Report
DESIGNER Dennis England
WRITER Beth Varcho

5 **DESIGN FIRM** Inside Out Design, New York, NY
CLIENT International Paper
PROJECT 2000 Annual Report
ART DIRECTOR Brian Wu
DESIGNER Stephen Loges
PHOTOGRAPHER Jack Kenner

2

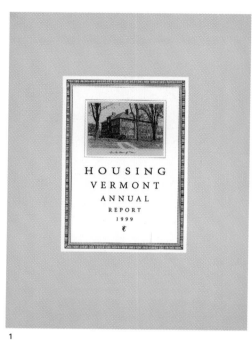

seamless

4

1

3

5

1 **DESIGN FIRM** Karin Johnson Design, Burlington, VT
  CLIENT Housing Vermont
  PROJECT Annual Report 1999
  ART DIRECTOR Karin T. Johnson
  DESIGNER Karin T. Johnson

2 **DESIGN FIRM** Kym Abrams Design Inc., Chicago, IL
  CLIENT The Joyce Foundation
  PROJECT 1999 Annual Report
  ART DIRECTOR Kym Abrams
  DESIGNER Ryan Pikkel

3 **DESIGN FIRM** Leimer Cross Design, Seattle, WA
  CLIENT Onyx Software
  PROJECT Onyx Business Value Onyx Customer Value
  ART DIRECTOR Kerry Leimer
  DESIGNER Kerry Leimer
  PHOTOGRAPHER Eric Myer

4 **DESIGN FIRM** Leimer Cross Design, Seattle, WA
  CLIENT b Square
  PROJECT b square Framework for X
  ART DIRECTOR Kerry Leimer
  DESIGNER Kerry Leimer
  PHOTOGRAPHER Eric Myer

5 **DESIGN FIRM** Leimer Cross Design, Seattle, WA
  CLIENT Esterline Technologies
  PROJECT Esterline 2000 It Comes Down to This
  ART DIRECTOR Kerry Leimer
  DESIGNER Kerry Leimer
  PHOTOGRAPHER Jeff Corwin

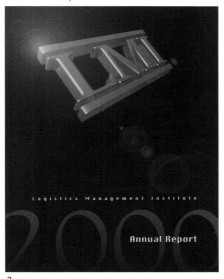

1

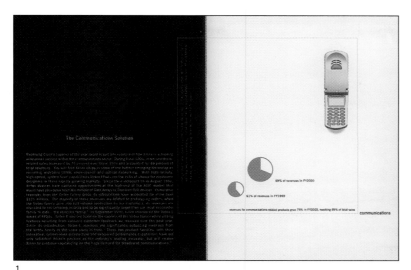

Microsoft_2000

2

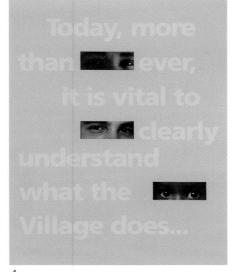

3

4

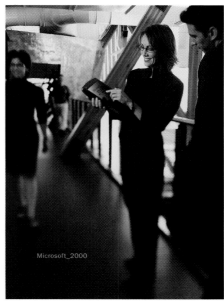

5

6

1 **DESIGN FIRM** Leimer Cross Design, Seattle, WA
CLIENT Xilinx, Inc.
PROJECT everything xilinx
ART DIRECTOR Kerry Leimer
DESIGNER Kerry Leimer
PHOTOGRAPHER Tyler Boley

2 **DESIGN FIRM** Leimer Cross Design, Seattle, WA
CLIENT Microsoft
PROJECT 2000 Annual Report
ART DIRECTOR Kerry Leimer
DESIGNER Kerry Leimer
PHOTOGRAPHER Eric Myer

3 **DESIGN FIRM** LMI, McLean, VA
PROJECT 2000 Annual Report
ART DIRECTORS Suzan Gibson/Kathy Myers
DESIGNER Suzan Gibson
PHOTOGRAPHERS Jim Douglas/Katherine Lambert
ILLUSTRATOR Brian Jensen

4 **DESIGN FIRM** Mason Design, Simsbury, CT
CLIENT Village for Families and Children Inc.
PROJECT Annual Report 99/00
ART DIRECTOR Ken Mason
DESIGNER Ken Mason
PHOTOGRAPHER Philip Fortune

5 **DESIGN FIRM** Meta-4 Design, Inc., Chicago, IL
CLIENT The Manitowoc Company
PROJECT The Right Moves
ART DIRECTOR Fred Biliter
DESIGNER Fred Biliter
PHOTOGRAPHERS Gary Yealon, Horizon Productions
ILLUSTRATOR J. Lenz

6 **DESIGN FIRM** Meta-4 Design, Inc., Chicago, IL
CLIENT The Allstate Corporation
PROJECT Making Change Happen 2000
ART DIRECTOR Jan Gulley
DESIGNERS Jan Gulley, Eugine Casis
PHOTOGRAPHERS Jean Moss, Andy Goodwin

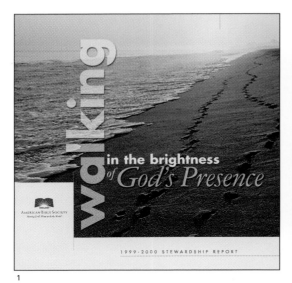

1

2

3

4

"On average, 1983 through 1996, the annual all-milk price was 31 cents a hundredweight higher than it would have been had there not been a mandatory 15 cent-per-hundredweight advertising check-off program. ...Therefore, nationally, dairy farmers spent 15 cents a hundred to make 31.

Not a bad return."

"...From 1996 through 1998...each dollar invested in generic fluid milk and cheese advertising by dairy farmers...returned $4.61, on average, in net revenue to farmers."

Quadruple the return.

Hoard's Dairyman *

5

1 **DESIGN FIRM** Mickey Moore and Associates, Charlottesville, VA
CLIENT American Bible Society
PROJECT 1999-2000 Annual Report
ART DIRECTOR Mickey Moore
DESIGNER Mickey Moore

2 **DESIGN FIRM** Nestor.Stermole VCG, New York, NY
CLIENT American Museum of Natural History
PROJECT Annual Report 1998-99
ART DIRECTOR Rick Stermole
DESIGNER Marc Levitt
PHOTOGRAPHER Dennis Finnin

3 **DESIGN FIRM** Nufolio, Inc., New York, NY
CLIENT The Town and Country Trust
PROJECT Annual Report 2000
ART DIRECTOR Nancy Merish
DESIGNER Nancy Merish

4 **DESIGN FIRM** Page Designs, Inc., Burlington, VT
CLIENT Vermont Agency of Natural Resources
PROJECT Environment 2001
ART DIRECTOR Terri Parent
DESIGNER Jennifer Karp Adrian

5 **DESIGN FIRM** Phinney/Bischoff Design House, Seattle, WA
CLIENT Washington Dairy Farmers Association
PROJECT Annual Report
ART DIRECTOR Leslie Phinney
DESIGNER Karin Harris

1

"We are relentless," he said.

Scenes from life at PECO Energy.

2

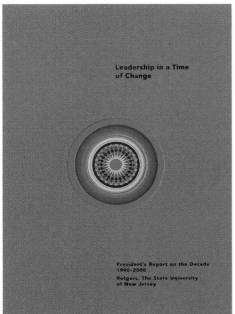

Quaker Chemical Corporation

1999 Annual Report

We **stand out**

by delivering

everywhere the best

from anywhere.

3

Pegasus Communications
2000 Summary Annual Report

BRINGING DIGITAL HOME

4

Leadership in a Time
of Change

President's Report on the Decade
1990-2000

Rutgers, The State University
of New Jersey

5

1 **DESIGN FIRM** RainCastle Communications, Inc., Newton, MA
   CLIENT Boston Scientific
   PROJECT 2000 Annual Report
   ART DIRECTOR Tony Catlin
   DESIGNER Tony Catlin
   PHOTOGRAPHER John Rae

2 **DESIGN FIRM** Rector Communications, Inc., Philadelphia, PA
   CLIENT Peco Energy Company
   PROJECT 1999 Annual Report
   ART DIRECTOR Cecile Hu
   DESIGNER Cecile Hu
   PHOTOGRAPHER Marc Carter
   COPYWRITER Don McCown

3 **DESIGN FIRM** Rector Communications, Inc., Philadelphia, PA
   CLIENT Quaker Chemical Corporation
   PROJECT 1999 Annual Report
   ART DIRECTOR Cecile Hu
   DESIGNER Cecile Hu
   PHOTOGRAPHER Ed Eckstein
   COPYWRITER Don McCown
   ILLUSTRATOR Doug Ross

4 **DESIGN FIRM** Robert Webster Inc., New York, NY
   CLIENT Pegasus Communications
   PROJECT 2000 Summary Annual Report
   ART DIRECTOR Michael DeVoursney
   PHOTOGRAPHER Preston Lyon

5 **DESIGN FIRM** Rutgers, The State University of New Jersey, New Brunswick, NJ
   CLIENT Rutgers Office of the President
   PROJECT President's Report 1990-2000
   ART DIRECTOR Joanne Dus-Zastrow
   DESIGNER Joanne Dus-Zastrow

1

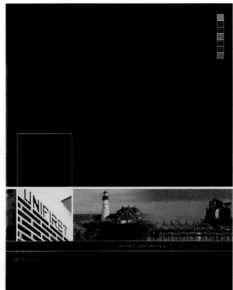

2

3

4

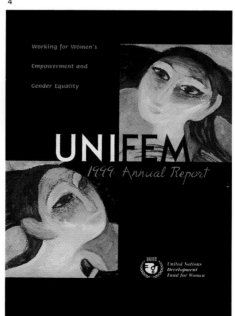

5

1 **DESIGN FIRM** Scana Corporation, Columbia, SC
PROJECT 2000 Annual Report
ART DIRECTOR Chris Merck
DESIGNER Chris Merck
PHOTOGRAPHER George Fulton Imagery

2 **DESIGN FIRM** SCK Design Inc., Cleveland, OH
CLIENT Unifirst Corporation
PROJECT Annual Report 2000
DESIGNER Leo Kosir
PHOTOGRAPHER Mike Steinberg

3 **DESIGN FIRM** SCK Design Inc., Cleveland, OH
CLIENT Century Business Services, Inc.
PROJECT Annual Report 2000
DESIGNER Leo Kosir

4 **DESIGN FIRM** Siren Design, Inc., Tenafly, NJ
CLIENT Varian Semiconductor Equipment
PROJECT Annual Report
ART DIRECTOR Joan Kristensen
DESIGNER Joan Kristensen
ILLUSTRATOR Joan Kristensen

5 **DESIGN FIRM** Stephanie Blackman Design,
New York, NY
CLIENT UNIFEM (United Nations)
PROJECT 1999 Annual Report
ART DIRECTOR Stephanie Blackman
DESIGNER Stephanie Blackman

1

2

3

4

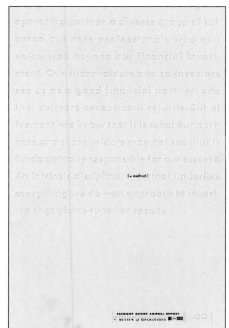

5

1 **DESIGN FIRM** Sundberg & Associates, New York, NY
CLIENT Fox Entertainment Group
PROJECT Annual Report
DESIGNER Doug Banquer

2 **DESIGN FIRM** t.a. design, Hamilton, NJ
CLIENT Community Medical Center
PROJECT Report to Community
ART DIRECTOR T. A. Hahn
DESIGNER T. A. Hahn
PHOTOGRAPHER Joe Cornish, Peter Olson

3 **DESIGN FIRM** Ted Bertz Graphic Design, Inc., Middletown, CT
CLIENT Harris Corporation
PROJECT Annual Report 2000
ART DIRECTOR Ted Bertz
DESIGNER Andrew Wessels
PHOTOGRAPHER Ted Kawalerski

4 **DESIGN FIRM** Ted Bertz Graphic Design, Inc., Middletown, CT
CLIENT Bausch & Lomb
PROJECT Annual Report 2000
ART DIRECTOR Ted Bertz
DESIGNER Richard Uccello
PHOTOGRAPHER Timothy Toal

5 **DESIGN FIRM** The Leonhardt Group, Seattle, WA
CLIENT Fremont Group
PROJECT 2000 Annual Report
ART DIRECTORS Steve Watson, Lesley Feldman
DESIGNERS Steve Watson, Lesley Feldman
PHOTOGRAPHER Abrams Lacagnina

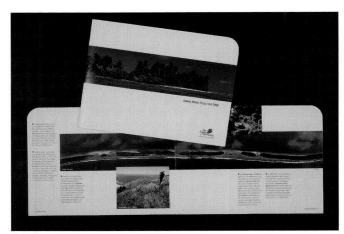

1

2

3

4

5

1 **DESIGN FIRM** The Nature Conservancy, Arlington, VA
PROJECT 2000 Annual Report
ART DIRECTOR Miya Su Rowe
DESIGNER Miya Su Rowe

2 **DESIGN FIRM** Three & Associates, Inc., Cincinnati, OH
CLIENT Federated Department Stores, Inc.
PROJECT 2000 Annual Report
ART DIRECTORS Ted Knapke, Gordon Cotton
DESIGNER Ted Knapke
PHOTOGRAPHER Trepal Photography
ILLUSTRATOR Ted Knapke

3 **DESIGN FIRM** Three-Five Systems, Inc., Tempe, AZ
PROJECT 1999 Annual Report
ART DIRECTOR Kimberly S. Bridgford
DESIGNER Kimberly S. Bridgford
PHOTOGRAPHERS Rick Raymond, Mark Culbertson

4 **DESIGN FIRM** VCG, New York, NY
CLIENT Curtiss Wright Corporation
PROJECT 2000 Annual Report
ART DIRECTOR Eric Teng
DESIGNER Rachael Nass
PHOTOGRAPHER John Rae

5 **DESIGN FIRM** VCG, New York, NY
CLIENT The Robert Wood Johnson Foundation
PROJECT 1999 Annual Report
ART DIRECTOR Eric Teng
DESIGNER Jane Margolis
PHOTOGRAPHER Roger Tully

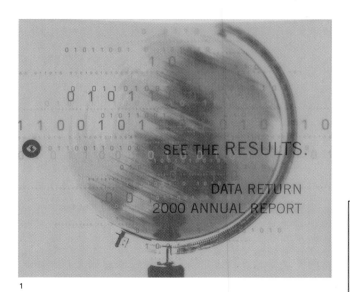

1

3

2

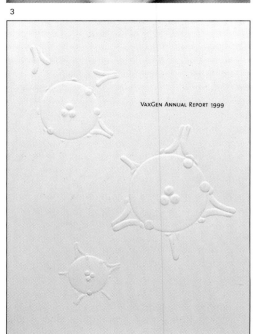

4

1 **DESIGN FIRM** VCG, New York, NY
  CLIENT Data Return
  PROJECT 2000 Annual Report
  ART DIRECTOR Eric Teng
  DESIGNER Patrick Durgin-Bruce

2 **DESIGN FIRM** VIA Marketing and Design, Inc., New York, NY
  CLIENT The Limited Inc.
  PROJECT 2000 Annual Report
  ART DIRECTOR Johan Vipper
  DESIGNER Johan Vipper
  PHOTOGRAPHERS Walter Chin, Dominique Isserman,
  Philip Dixon, Kit Latham
  ILLUSTRATOR Izak

3 **DESIGN FIRM** VIA Marketing and Design, Inc., New York, NY
  CLIENT Intimate Brands Inc.
  PROJECT 2000 Annual Report
  ART DIRECTOR Johan Vipper
  DESIGNER Ruth Diener
  PHOTOGRAPHERS Tim Walker, Russell James, Rita Moss,
  Dominique Isserman, Dan Lecca, Bruce Wolf, Sandra Johnson
  ILLUSTRATOR Izak

4 **DESIGN FIRM** Vinje Design, Inc., El Cerrito, CA
  CLIENT VaxGen, Inc.
  PROJECT 1999 Annual Report
  ART DIRECTOR Andreas Keller
  DESIGNER Andrea Keller
  PHOTOGRAPHER Jim Karageorge
  ILLUSTRATOR Neil Brennan

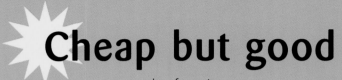

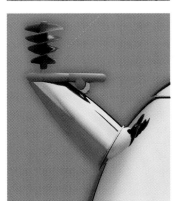

a little **twist** with your tea

michael graves design · spinning whistle teakettle 34.99 target.com

The Single-Wire Solution

VistaNET 2.0 is a single-wire network architecture that enables seamless connectivity to existing Ethernet-based systems and higher level processes. With VistaNET 2.0 all process analytical equipment can share the same network for data exchange — with control systems, plant engineers, maintenance engineers and other data users — in a true distributed network architecture. VistaNET 2.0 provides all users with a common platform for data collection, presentation and analysis.

- Apply with ABB Analytical & Third-Party Analyzers
- Connect to LAN, Plant LAN & WAN
- Connect to Higher-Level Processes
- Uses Existing Cabling
- Reduce Costs
- OPC Awareness Built-In
- ABB Analytical Support — Worldwide

VistaNET 2.0
Integrated Process Analyzer
Network Architecture

Connect with ABB Analytical

For complete information about VistaNET 2.0 contact any ABB Analytical facility worldwide. Our world team members can help you determine the best way to capitalize on this powerful new architecture, and provide complete assistance as you apply VistaNET 2.0 to your operation.

ABB Automation
Analytical Division

Visit our website at www.abb.com/analytical for additional information.

Production – Lewisburg · WV USA 1.304.947.4368 · Bomem – Quebec Canada 1.418.877.2944
Extrel – Pittsburgh PA USA 1.412.963.7530 · CGA – Frankfurt Germany 49.6196.800.0
Systems Integration – Houston TX USA 1.713.460.9541 · Telford Shropshire UK 44.1952.670.477
Sales – Americas 1.281.556.8102 · Bahrain 973.725977 · Benelux 31.15.616.9053 · China 86.10.6698.1809
France 33.3.87.18.74.00 · India 91.120.627.9927 · Italy 90.2.23928751 · Singapore 65.768.7855

ABB

1

ANYWHERE.

YES, ANYWHERE.

Your properties don't confine themselves to a single state. So your defaults don't either. Now, you can turn to the title professionals skilled in refinance and equity loan default services for assistance with any property anywhere in the U.S.

With the National Default Title Services group of First American Lenders Advantage, you'll have one point of contact to handle your title-refund default needs — no matter where your properties are located. From loan analysis and foreclosure reports to the final resale and closing of REO property, our professionals are with you every step of the way.

Our vast database of property records — the industry's largest — combines with our title expertise to make services easy, in every state in the nation. Now, we're ready to do the same for you...anywhere.

Call us. We do it. It's done.

LENDERS ADVANTAGE

First American Title Insurance Company
2 First American Way
Santa Ana, CA 92702
National Default Title Services (800) 255-3693
www.firstam.com · NYSE FAF

NATIONAL DEFAULT TITLE SERVICES | Default Title Coordination | Property Reports | Online Title Tracking | Loan Modification
REO Services | TITLE INSURANCE AND SERVICES | REAL ESTATE INFORMATION AND SERVICES | CONSUMER INFORMATION AND SERVICES

4

KidFits™

Bringing Back Their Smiles

KidFits™ Pediatric arch supports offer gentle corrective control that is perfect for the little tikes. Face it: kids can be the toughest patients. They can't always communicate to you when enough is enough, leaving you to wonder whether you may have been too aggressive. How can you be sure without feedback? It's an unnerving predicament.

KidFits™ give you confidence because they contain no rigid plastics. They are made of EVA laminates, which gain their structural support through curvature and void-space fill. Gentle corrective control is what our arch supports are all about. Goldilocks said it best: "Not to hard, not to soft, just right."

KidFits™ come in a number of colors, sizes, and material combinations. They are easily heat adapted. They are modifiable and grindable. Adjust them easily to suit the needs of your little patients. Bring the smiles back to the faces of kids with achy feet!

NEW!

For More Information and a free sample, call 1-800-237-2267

ACOR ORTHOPAEDIC, INC.

18530 South Miles Parkway · Cleveland, OH 44128
ph: 800.237.2267 fax: 216.662.4547
www.acor.com
KidFits is a trademark of Acor Orthopaedic, Inc.

3

NOW YOU GET THE PICTURE.

Instantly. Clearly. With field service photos delivered at the speed of the Internet.

And this progressive, new online field services system lets you access far more than clear photos from your personal computer. You can place or cancel inspection and property preservation orders. View order status, history of prior completions and invoice information. Access critical management reports, including first-time vacancy, damaged properties, confirmation and conveyance completions. And then communicate easily with us via email.

We even bring you the only Internet field services site in the industry to provide HUD over-allowable and time-extension forms online.

So experience true efficiency, as the ease of the Internet combines with a national menu of hands-on field inspection and property preservation services.

Call us. We do it. It's done.

First American Field Services

800-680-9273
www.firstam.com
NYSE FAF

REAL ESTATE INFORMATION AND SERVICES | Appraisal Services | Credit Reporting | Flood Determinations | Loan Document Preparation |
Real Estate Tax Reporting | Lender-placed Insurance | Flood Compliance | Field Services | Loan Servicing Systems | Tax Valuation | Default Management |
Loss Mitigation | Database Information and Services | TITLE INSURANCE SERVICES | CONSUMER INFORMATION AND SERVICES

5

1

2

3

5

local real estate, globally

commercial real estate in over 250 locations worldwide   www.colliers.com

4

1 **DESIGN FIRM** Gammon Ragonesi Associates, New York, NY
   CLIENT Skyy Spirits
   PROJECT Inizio Magazine for Campari 2001 Edition
   ART DIRECTOR Mary Ragonesi
   DESIGNER Mary Ragonesi
   PHOTOGRAPHER Greg Lord

2 **DESIGN FIRM** Gauger & Silva Associates, San Francisco, CA
   CLIENT Shea Homes
   PROJECT Time Series
   ART DIRECTORS Kait Courlang, David Gauger
   DESIGNER Kait Courlang

3 **DESIGN FIRM** Greco Ethridge Group, New York, NY
   CLIENT Information Week
   PROJECT Erase Doubt
   ART DIRECTOR Charles Hively
   DESIGNER Charles Hively
   PHOTOGRAPHER Frederik Broden

4 **DESIGN FIRM** Greenfield/Belser Ltd., Washington, DC
   CLIENT Colliers International
   PROJECT Stamps Diorama
   ART DIRECTOR Burkey Belser
   DESIGNERS Charlyne Fabi, Burkey Belser

5 **DESIGN FIRM** Greenfield/Belser Ltd., Washington, DC
   CLIENT Pillsbury Winthrop
   PROJECT Wake Up/Coffee Ad
   ART DIRECTORS Burkey Belser, Charlyne Fabi
   DESIGNER Charlyne Fabi
   ILLUSTRATOR Jacey

1

2

3

4

5

1 DESIGN FIRM Harman Consumer Group, Woodbury, NY
CLIENT Infinity Systems
PROJECT Ad Insert
ART DIRECTOR Bob Abbatecola
DESIGNER Chris Rugen
PHOTOGRAPHER Josh McClure

2 DESIGN FIRM Harte-Hanks, Langhome, PA
CLIENT Great-West/ADA Insurance Plans
PROJECT Plunge
ART DIRECTOR Hannah Leader
DESIGNER Joe Brizzi

3 DESIGN FIRM Imagine That Design Studio, San Francisco, CA
CLIENT Sakura of America
PROJECT Power to Express Pink
ART DIRECTOR Patti Mangan
DESIGNER Bill Owen
PHOTOGRAPHER Rod Spicer

4 DESIGN FIRM Inside Out Communications, Holliston, MA
CLIENT Revit Technology
PROJECT Dialogue Architectural Record
ART DIRECTOR Matt Lynch
DESIGNER Matt Lynch

5 DESIGN FIRM Keiler & Company, Farmington, CT
CLIENT Crane's
PROJECT Experience Pure Harmony
ART DIRECTOR Liz Dzilenski
DESIGNER Liz Dzilenski
ILLUSTRATOR Rowan Barnes-Murphy

1

A Gallery of Business Classics

A Cross-Market Portfolio
Built to Serve
Decisionmakers

When your client
needs target-market
impact, choose the
cross-industry leaders
that invented
integrated marketing
solutions.

**Printing, Packaging,
& Creative Group**

3

2

4

1 **DESIGN FIRM** Michael Indresano Photography, Boston, MA
  PROJECT Lawyer Malloy
  ART DIRECTOR Tom Laidlaw
  DESIGNER Jonathan Grove
  PHOTOGRAPHER Michael Indresano

2 **DESIGN FIRM** Michael Indresano Photography, Boston, MA
  CLIENT Sport Magazine
  PROJECT Nomar Garciaparra
  PHOTOGRAPHER Michael Indresano

3 **DESIGN FIRM** Old Bergen Design, Jersey City, NJ
  CLIENT Cahners
  PROJECT A Gallery of Classics
  ART DIRECTOR Kenneth Quail
  DESIGNER Kenneth Quail
  ILLUSTRATOR Kenneth Quail

4 **DESIGN FIRM** Old Bergen Design, Jersey City, NJ
  CLIENT Cahners
  PROJECT World Group
  ART DIRECTOR Kenneth Quail
  DESIGNER Kenneth Quail

1

2

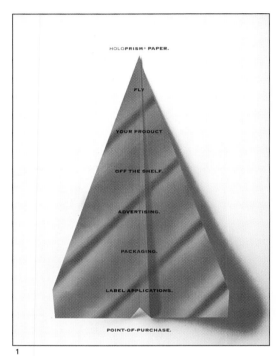

4

3

1 **DESIGN FIRM** Proma Technologies, Franklin, MA
  PROJECT Airplane Ad
  ART DIRECTOR Rich Kerstein
  DESIGNER Darlene Chang

2 **DESIGN FIRM** The Humane Society of the United States, Gaithersburg, MD
  PROJECT Looking for Animal Information on the Web?
  ART DIRECTOR Paula Jaworski
  DESIGNER Daniel Clohan

3 **DESIGN FIRM** The Humane Society of the United States, Gaithersburg, MD
  PROJECT It's A Jungle Out There
  ART DIRECTOR Paula Jaworski
  DESIGNER Daniel Clohan

4 **DESIGN FIRM** ZGraphics, Ltd., East Dundee, IL
  CLIENT Pactiv Corporation
  PROJECT Hefty Slide-Rite Ad Campaign
  ART DIRECTOR Joe Zeller
  DESIGNER Renee Clark
  PHOTOGRAPHER Don Guest Photography

1

2

3

1 **DESIGN FIRM** Bailey Design Group, Plymouth Meeting, PA
PROJECT Holiday Card
ART DIRECTOR Steve Perry
DESIGNERS Sean Costik, Steve Perry

2 **DESIGN FIRM** Bloomberg, Princeton, NJ
CLIENT The Metropolitan Museum of Art
PROJECT Jackie O./Vermeer Private Viewing Invite
ART DIRECTOR Sandy O'Connor
DESIGNER Holly Tienken

3 **DESIGN FIRM** Bloomberg, Princeton, NJ
CLIENT Bloomberg L.P.
PROJECT The White House Correspondents' Dinner Cocktail Party Invite
ART DIRECTOR Sandy O'Connor
DESIGNER Ann Walker

4 **DESIGN FIRM** Boston University, Boston, MA
PROJECT Ravinia
DESIGNER Wendy Garbarino
ILLUSTRATOR Tony Bennett

5 **DESIGN FIRM** Boston University, Boston, MA
PROJECT A Day of Art
DESIGNER Amy Osborne

4

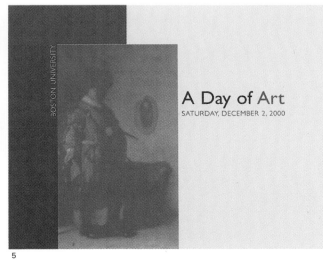

5

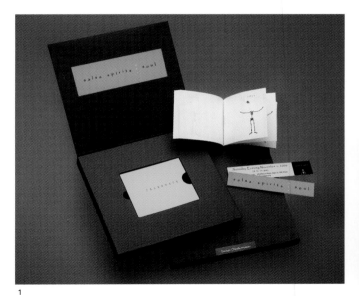

1

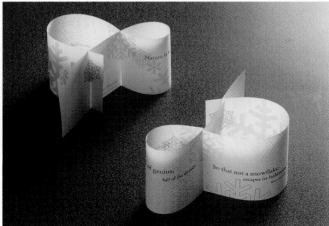

1 **DESIGN FIRM** Cisneros Design, Inc., Santa Fe, NM
CLIENT Georgia O'Keefe Museum
PROJECT Salsa Invitation
ART DIRECTOR Brian Hurshman
DESIGNER Brian Hurshman

2 **DESIGN FIRM** EPOS, Inc., Santa Monica, CA
PROJECT Christmas Card 2000
ART DIRECTOR Gabrielle Raumberger
DESIGNER Clifford Singontiko

3 **DESIGN FIRM** Flourish, Cleveland, OH
PROJECT Jingle and Mingle
ART DIRECTOR Jing Lauengco
DESIGNER Jing Lauengco
ILLUSTRATOR Jing Lauengco

4 **DESIGN FIRM** Ford & Earl Associates, Troy, MI
PROJECT 2000/2001 Holiday Card
ART DIRECTOR Bonnie Zielinski
DESIGNER Robin Olson
ILLUSTRATOR Robin Olson

5 **DESIGN FIRM** Getty Images, Seattle, WA
CLIENT Stone
PROJECT Naughty or Nice
ART DIRECTOR Michael Lindsay
DESIGNER Jen Covington
PHOTOGRAPHER Darren Robb

2

3

5

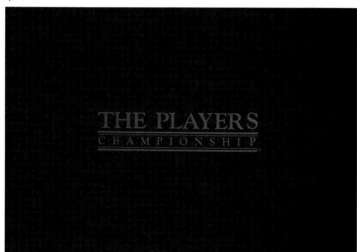

1 **DESIGN FIRM** Gill Fishman Associates, Cambridge, MA
CLIENT Gill Fishman Associates and Margolis and Fishman
PROJECT 1/1/1 Holiday Card
ART DIRECTOR Gill Fishman
DESIGNER Gill Fishman

2 **DESIGN FIRM** Greenfield/Belser Ltd., Washington, DC
CLIENT Orrick Herrington & Sutcliffe
PROJECT Holiday Card
ART DIRECTOR Burkey Belser
DESIGNER Jill Sasser
COPYWRITER Lise Anne Schwartz

3 **DESIGN FIRM** HardBall Sports, Jacksonville, FL
CLIENT PGA Tour
PROJECT The Players Gala Invitation
ART DIRECTOR Andy Gosendi
DESIGNERS Michael O'Connell, Andy Gosendi
PHOTOGRAPHER PGA Tour

4 **DESIGN FIRM** Hare Strigenz Design, Inc., Milwaukee, WI
CLIENT Quarles & Brady
PROJECT Evening in the Park Invitation
ART DIRECTOR Paula Hare
DESIGNER Jackie Cmkovich

5 **DESIGN FIRM** Household International Employee Communications, Prospect Heights, IL
CLIENT Household Human Resources
PROJECT Holiday Invite
ART DIRECTOR Chris Tomsic
DESIGNER Bob Zwolinski

1

2

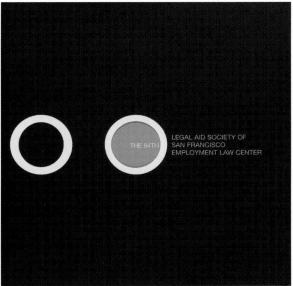

3

1 **DESIGN FIRM** ignition13 inc., Stamford, CT
CLIENT State University of New York - Purchase
PROJECT Friends of Music Invitation
DESIGNER ignition13 inc.

2 **DESIGN FIRM** Inter Group Communications, Pittsburgh, PA
CLIENT Fiserv
PROJECT 2001 Client Conference Invitational Brochure
ART DIRECTOR Kurt Valenta
DESIGNER Kurt Valenta
ILLUSTRATOR Kurt Valenta

3 **DESIGN FIRM** Ison Design, San Francisco, CA
CLIENT Legal Aid Society of San Francisco
DESIGNER Annabelle Ison

4 **DESIGN FIRM** John Kallio Graphic Design, New Haven, CT
CLIENT Connecticut Business & Industry Association
PROJECT GHO Invitation
ART DIRECTOR John Kallio
DESIGNER John Kallio

5 **DESIGN FIRM** Jones Design Group, Atlanta, GA
PROJECT Christmas/Holiday Card
ART DIRECTOR Vicky Jones
DESIGNERS Katherine Staggs, Julia Randell, Caroline McAlpine, Chris Miller

4

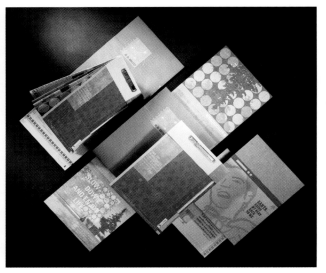

5

1

2

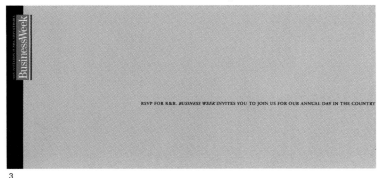

3

4

5

1 **DESIGN FIRM** Jowaisas Design, Cazenovia, NY
  CLIENT King & King Architects
  PROJECT See What We've Put Together Invitation
  DESIGNER Elizabeth Jowaisas
  PHOTOGRAPHER Joanne Cook

2 **DESIGN FIRM** Leibowitz Communications, New York, NY
  CLIENT Business Week
  PROJECT Le Colonial Invitation
  ART DIRECTOR Paul Leibowitz
  DESIGNER Rick Bargmann

3 **DESIGN FIRM** Leibowitz Communications, New York, NY
  CLIENT Business Week
  PROJECT Golf Invitation
  ART DIRECTOR Paul Leibowitz
  DESIGNER Rick Bargmann
  ILLUSTRATOR Rick Bargmann

4 **DESIGN FIRM** M. Farinella Design, Wayne, NJ
  PROJECT Greeting/Holiday Cards
  ART DIRECTOR Michelle Farinella
  DESIGNER Michelle Farinella
  ILLUSTRATOR Adriano Farinella

5 **DESIGN FIRM** Matousek Design, Los Angeles, CA
  CLIENT Pongo Productions
  PROJECT Holiday Card
  ART DIRECTOR Michael Matousek
  DESIGNER Michael Matousek
  STRUCTURAL ENGINEERING Eric Ward, Four Corners
  LOGO DESIGN Mark Fox

1

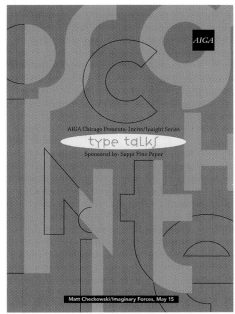

3

2

4

YOU'VE ENDURED THE PAIN.

5

1 **DESIGN FIRM** New Jersey State Aquarium at Camden, Camden, NJ
CLIENT New Jersey Academy for Aquatic Science
PROJECT FINtastic Invitation
ART DIRECTOR Monika Koval
DESIGNER Jennifer Warholak

2 **DESIGN FIRM** Oakwood DC, Manhattan Beach, CA
PROJECT Christmas Card
ART DIRECTOR Rick Delome
DESIGNER Alan Fisher

3 **DESIGN FIRM** Olver Dunlop Associates, Chicago, IL
CLIENT AIGA/Chicago
PROJECT Type Talks
ART DIRECTOR Julia Dunlop
DESIGNER Jill Tanzer

4 **DESIGN FIRM** Rule 29, Elgin, IL
CLIENT Solid Rock Foundation
PROJECT Alice Cooper 2000 Celebrity Golf Am Invite
ART DIRECTORS Justin Ahrens, Jim Boborci
DESIGNERS Justin Ahrens, Jim Boborci
PHOTOGRAPHER James Leland
ILLUSTRATORS Justin Ahrens, Jim Boborci

5 **DESIGN FIRM** Sage Marcom, Inc., Liverpool, NY
CLIENT Syracuse Ad Club
PROJECT 2001 Addy Awards Invitation
ART DIRECTOR Thomas Gilhooly
DESIGNER Thomas Gilhooly
PHOTOGRAPHER James Scherzi
ILLUSTRATOR Karanya Aksornkoae

2

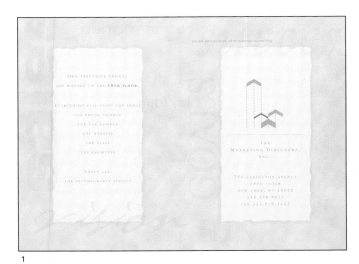

1

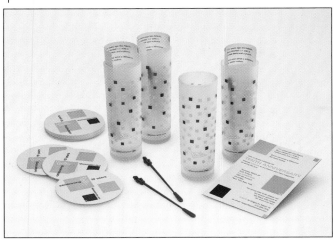

3

5

1 **DESIGN FIRM** Sherman Advertising, New York, NY
CLIENT The Marketing Directors
PROJECT Moving Announcement
ART DIRECTOR Sharon Elaine Lloyd
DESIGNER Sharon Elaine Lloyd

2 **DESIGN FIRM** Simon Design, New York, NY
CLIENT Ms. Foundation for Women
PROJECT Carolines or Bust!
ART DIRECTOR Karen Simon
DESIGNER Karen Simon

3 **DESIGN FIRM** SJI Associates Inc., New York, NY
PROJECT Anniversary Party Invitation
ART DIRECTOR Jill Vinitsky
DESIGNERS Ilene Block, Marie Coons

4 **DESIGN FIRM** Stan Gellman Graphic Design, St. Louis, MO
CLIENT University of Illinois Foundation
PROJECT The Power of Thought 65th Annual Meeting
ART DIRECTOR Barry Tilson
DESIGNER Mike Donovan
PHOTOGRAPHER University of Illinois

5 **DESIGN FIRM** The Alumni Association of the University of Michigan, Ann Arbor, MI
PROJECT Distinguished Alumni Service Award 2001
ART DIRECTOR Donna M. Malski
DESIGNER Donna M. Malski

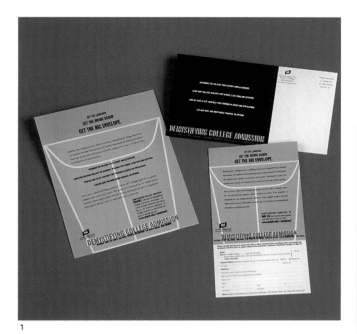

1

3

2

4

1 **DESIGN FIRM** The Alumni Association of the University of Michigan, Ann Arbor, MI
PROJECT Demystifying College Admission Campaign
ART DIRECTOR Donna M. Malski
DESIGNER Donna M. Malski
ILLUSTRATOR Donna M. Malski

2 **DESIGN FIRM** Towers Perrin, Chicago, IL
PROJECT Creative Media Holiday Cards
ART DIRECTORS Fawn Roth Winick, Scott May
DESIGNER Media Consultants
PHOTOGRAPHER Media Consultants
ILLUSTRATOR Media Consultants

3 **DESIGN FIRM** Willey Brothers, Inc., Rochester, NH
PROJECT Pebble Beach Thought Advance 2000 Invitation
ART DIRECTOR Betsy Bennett
DESIGNER Betsy Bennett

4 **DESIGN FIRM** Zermatt, Luling, LA
CLIENT Cirque Du Soleil
PROJECT Look Closely
ART DIRECTOR Tracy McLaughlin
DESIGNER Matt Touchard
ILLUSTRATOR Matt Touchard

for your 15 minutes of fame

INTRODUCING 3 LEVELS OF COMPS TO SATISFY
YOUR BUDGET AND DEADLINE

www.photobitioncomp.com   800 848 7716

BOOKS
NEWSLETTERS
PUBLICATIONS

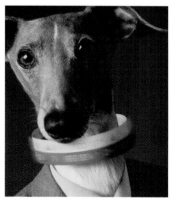

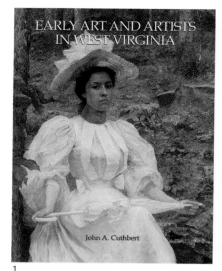

1

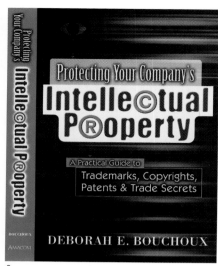

2

3

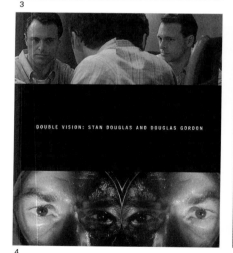

4

5

6

1 **DESIGN FIRM** Alcorn Publication Design, Graeagle, CA
 CLIENT West Virginia University Press
 PROJECT Early Art and Artists in West Virginia
 ART DIRECTOR David Alcorn
 DESIGNER David Alcorn

2 **DESIGN FIRM** AMA Creative, Watertown, MA
 CLIENT AMACOM
 PROJECT Protecting Your Company's
 Intellectual Property
 ART DIRECTORS Bob Chen, Cathleen Ouderkirk
 DESIGNER Bob Chen

3 **DESIGN FIRM** DeVa Design, Manhattan Beach, CA
 CLIENT MGM Grand
 PROJECT Viva Il Sogno
 ART DIRECTOR Debra Valencia
 DESIGNER Debra Valencia
 PHOTOGRAPHER Tim Street-Porter

4 **DESIGN FIRM** Dia Center for the Arts, New York, NY
 PROJECT Double Vision: Stan Douglas and
 Douglas Gordon
 DESIGNER Bethany Johns
 ILLUSTRATORS Stan Douglas, Douglas Gordon

5 **DESIGN FIRM** H.A.R. Marketing,
 Morro Bay, CA
 CLIENT Nikolai Alexandrov
 PROJECT The Heart of the Butterfly
 ART DIRECTOR Hilary A. Rinaldi
 DESIGNER Hilary A. Rinaldi

6 **DESIGN FIRM** J. Paul Getty Trust-Publications
 Services, Los Angeles, CA
 CLIENT J. Paul Getty Museum
 PROJECT Degas Sketchbook
 DESIGNER Kurt Hauser
 PHOTOGRAPHER Lou Meluso

1

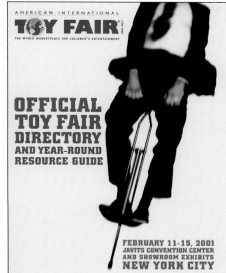

2

3

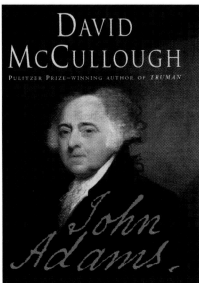

4

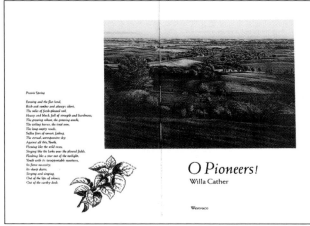

5

6

1 **DESIGN FIRM** Miriello Grafico, Inc., San Diego, CA
CLIENT Qualcomm
PROJECT Phil White Retirement Book
ART DIRECTOR Michelle Aranda
DESIGNER Michelle Aranda

2 **DESIGN FIRM** Old Bergen Design, Jersey City, NJ
CLIENT Toy Manufacturers
PROJECT Toy Fair Directory
ART DIRECTOR Kenneth Quail
DESIGNER Kenneth Quail

3 **DESIGN FIRM** Stuart Silberman Graphic Design,
San Francisco, CA
CLIENT Harper Collins, Jack Griggs
PROJECT The FeederWatcher's Guide to Bird Feeding
DESIGNER Stuart L. Silberman

4 **DESIGN FIRM** The Shamrock Companies Inc., Westlake, OH
CLIENT Ursuline College
PROJECT Development Book
ART DIRECTOR John Bennett
DESIGNER Lori Leiter

5 **DESIGN FIRM** Wendell Minor Design, Washington, CT
CLIENT Simon & Schuster
PROJECT John Adams
ART DIRECTOR Michael Accordino
DESIGNER Wendell Minor
ILLUSTRATOR Wendell Minor

6 **DESIGN FIRM** Westvaco Corporation, New York, NY
PROJECT O Pioneers!
ART DIRECTOR John Boyd
DESIGNER Karen M. Elder
ILLUSTRATOR James D. Butler

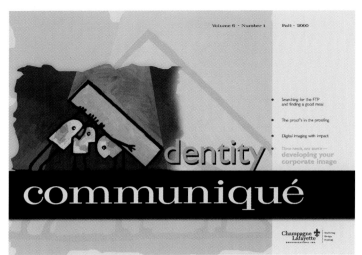

1 **DESIGN FIRM** Ann Hill Communications,
San Rafael, CA
CLIENT SFECA
PROJECT S.F. Electric Times Newsletter - Volume VI
ART DIRECTOR Greg Kerwin
DESIGNER Jack Zoog
PHOTOGRAPHER Steve Maruta
ILLUSTRATOR Scott Woodworth

2 **DESIGN FIRM** Champagne/Lafayette
Communications Inc., Natick, MA
CLIENT Communiqué
PROJECT Fall 2000
ART DIRECTOR Linda Luiso
DESIGNER Janet Ireland

3 **DESIGN FIRM** Dennis Johnson Design, Oakland, CA
CLIENT Lucile Packard Foundation For
Children's Health
PROJECT Packard Children's News, Winter 2000
ART DIRECTOR Dennis Johnson
DESIGNER Dennis Johnson
PHOTOGRAPHER Steve Fisch

4 **DESIGN FIRM** HardBall Sports, Jacksonville, FL
CLIENT University Club
PROJECT Newsletter (Monthly)
ART DIRECTOR Andy Gosendi
DESIGNERS Andy Gosendi, Michael O'Connell

5 **DESIGN FIRM** Household International Employee
Communications, Prospect Heights, IL
CLIENT Household Employee Communications
PROJECT Household Today Newsletter
ART DIRECTOR Chris Tomsic
DESIGNER Bob Zwolinski
ILLUSTRATOR Bob Zwolinski

1

2

3

4

5

1 **DESIGN FIRM** JA Design Solutions, Coppell, TX
CLIENT TXU
PROJECT TXU View-Employee Newsletter
ART DIRECTOR Jean Ashenfelter
DESIGNER Jean Ashenfelter

2 **DESIGN FIRM** Jacqueline Barrett Design Inc., Oceanport, NJ
CLIENT Merck & Co., Inc.
PROJECT George W. Merck Tribute
DESIGNER Jacqueline Barrett

3 **DESIGN FIRM** Litton Integrated Systems, Agoura Hills, CA
PROJECT Inside ISD
ART DIRECTOR Ellen Gilbert
DESIGNER Linda Shalack
PHOTOGRAPHER Mike Marcus

4 **DESIGN FIRM** Orbit Integrated, Hockessin, DE
PROJECT Thought Process Newsletter
ART DIRECTORS Bill Harris, Jack Harris
DESIGNER Mark Miller

5 **DESIGN FIRM** Philip Morris Management Corp.,
New York, NY
CLIENT Philip Morris
PROJECT TrendTracker
ART DIRECTOR Walter Kryshak

1 **DESIGN FIRM** Philip Morris Management Corp.,
New York, NY
CLIENT Philip Morris
PROJECT Philip Morris Focus
ART DIRECTOR Walter Kryshak
DESIGNER Walter Kryshak

2 **DESIGN FIRM** Proma Technologies, Franklin, MA
PROJECT Illuminations
ART DIRECTOR Darlene Chang
DESIGNER Darlene Chang
PHOTOGRAPHER Durvin & Co.

3 **DESIGN FIRM** Shelby Designs & Illustrates, Oakland, CA
CLIENT Franciscan Winery
PROJECT Terroir Newsletter
ART DIRECTOR Shelby Tupper
DESIGNER Shelby Tupper

4 **DESIGN FIRM** Smith Design Associates, Bloomfield, NJ
CLIENT Smith Design Associates
PROJECT The Right Side
ART DIRECTOR James C. Smith
DESIGNER Jeffrey Drake
ILLUSTRATORS Robert Steinman, Michael Altman

5 **DESIGN FIRM** The College Board, New York, NY
PROJECT The Bulletin Board
ART DIRECTOR Julia Selinger
DESIGNER Julia Selinger
PHOTOGRAPHER John Uliery

3

2

1

4

5

1

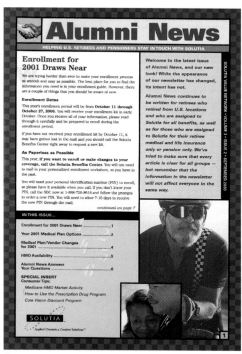

2

3

4

1 **DESIGN FIRM** Thompson Studio, Doylestown, PA
CLIENT Butler International/Bluestorm
PROJECT Stormwatch Newsletter
ART DIRECTOR Emily Thompson
DESIGNER Emily Thompson

2 **DESIGN FIRM** Towers Perrin, Southfield, MI
CLIENT Solutia Inc.
PROJECT Alumni News
DESIGNER Rebecca Deason

3 **DESIGN FIRM** Westvaco Corporation,
New York, NY
PROJECT FYI-A Guide to Westvaco's Global
Package Resources
ART DIRECTOR Karen M. Elder
DESIGNER Karen M. Elder

4 **DESIGN FIRM** ZGraphics, Ltd., East Dundee, IL
CLIENT Contempo Design
PROJECT Newsletter
ART DIRECTOR Joe Zeller
DESIGNER Kris Martinez Farrell

2

1

3

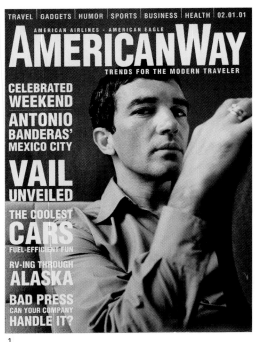

4

1 **DESIGN FIRM** American Way, Fort Worth, TX
PROJECT February 2001 Cover
ART DIRECTOR Gilberto Mejia
DESIGNER Charles Stone

2 **DESIGN FIRM** American Way, Fort Worth, TX
PROJECT Coup D'Etat
ART DIRECTOR Gilberto Mejia
DESIGNER Charles Stone
PHOTOGRAPHER Robin Hill

3 **DESIGN FIRM** American Way, Fort Worth, TX
PROJECT So Near, So Far Away
ART DIRECTOR Gilberto Mejia
DESIGNER Gilberto Mejia
PHOTOGRAPHER Jack Reznicki

4 **DESIGN FIRM** American Way, Fort Worth, TX
PROJECT Sgt. Pepper Revisited
ART DIRECTOR Gilberto Mejia
DESIGNERS Gilberto Mejia, Melanie Fowler

5 **DESIGN FIRM** American Way, Fort Worth, TX
PROJECT Island Escapes
ART DIRECTOR Gilberto Mejia
DESIGNER Gilberto Mejia

5

1

3

4

2

5

1 **DESIGN FIRM** American Way, Fort Worth, TX
PROJECT New Kind of Adventure
ART DIRECTOR Gilberto Mejia
DESIGNER Melanie Fowler
PHOTOGRAPHER Nathan Bilow

2 **DESIGN FIRM** Berkeley Lab-Public Information Dept., St. Paul, MN
CLIENT Berkeley Lab
PROJECT Highlights 1999-2000
ART DIRECTOR Niza Hanany
DESIGNER Niza Hanany
PHOTOGRAPHER Roy Kaltschmidt
EDITOR Pam Patterson
WRITERS Paul Preuss, Lynn Yarris

3 **DESIGN FIRM** Bloomberg, Princeton, NJ
CLIENT Wealth Manager
PROJECT December 2000/January 2001
ART DIRECTOR Laura Zaretz
DESIGNERS Laura Zaretz, Bea McDonald

4 **DESIGN FIRM** Bloomberg, Princeton, NJ
CLIENT Wealth Manager
PROJECT October 2000
ART DIRECTOR Laura Zaretz
DESIGNERS Laura Zaretz, Bea McDonald

5 **DESIGN FIRM** Bloomberg, Princeton, NJ
CLIENT Wealth Manager
PROJECT May 2000
ART DIRECTOR Laura Zaretz
DESIGNERS Laura Zaretz, Bea McDonald

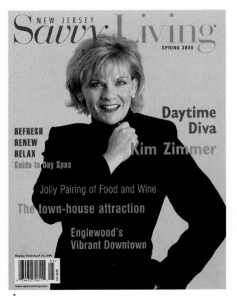

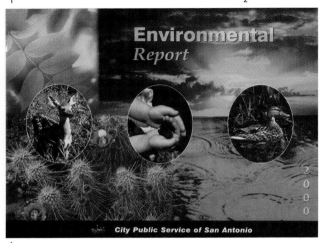

1 **DESIGN FIRM** C&C Graphics, Malverne, NY
CLIENT CTB Publishing
PROJECT New Jersey Savvy Living Spring 2000
CREATIVE DIRECTOR Lisa L. Cangemi
DESIGNER Lisa L. Cangemi
PHOTOGRAPHER Lane Pederson

2 **DESIGN FIRM** Cahners Business Information, Newton, MA
CLIENT Supply Chain Management Review
PROJECT Time Management & The Supply Chain
ART DIRECTOR Keisha Donovan
ILLUSTRATOR Susan Leopold

3 **DESIGN FIRM** Children's Hospital of Pittsburgh, Pittsburgh, PA
PROJECT Colors
ART DIRECTOR Michael Tarquinio
DESIGNER Michael Tarquinio
PHOTOGRAPHERS Andrea London, Ric Evans, Terry Clark, Bill Exler

4 **DESIGN FIRM** City Public Service, San Antonio, TX
CLIENT PROJECT Environmental Report 2000
ART DIRECTOR David Howard
DESIGNER Melissa Oaks

5 **DESIGN FIRM** CXO Media, Inc. (CIO & Darwin), Framingham, MA
CLIENT CIO Magazine
PROJECT Why We're Still Talking...
ART DIRECTOR Mary Lester
DESIGNER Kaajal Asher
ILLUSTRATOR John Ritter

1

2

3

4

5

1 DESIGN FIRM CXO Media, Inc. (CIO & Darwin), Framingham, MA
CLIENT CIO Magazine
PROJECT High Anxiety
ART DIRECTOR Mary Lester
DESIGNER Owen Edwards
PHOTOGRAPHER Marcos Lujas

2 DESIGN FIRM CXO Media, Inc. (CIO & Darwin), Framingham, MA
CLIENT Darwin Magazine
PROJECT Talking the Talk
ART DIRECTOR Mary Lester
DESIGNER Terri Haas, Kaajal Asher
ILLUSTRATOR Josef Gast

3 DESIGN FIRM CXO Media, Inc. (CIO & Darwin), Framingham, MA
CLIENT Darwin Magazine
PROJECT Cover
ART DIRECTOR Mary Lester
DESIGNER Terri Haas
PHOTOGRAPHER Furnald Gray

4 DESIGN FIRM Dever Designs, Laurel, MD
CLIENT American Style Magazine
PROJECT Jewels of Art
ART DIRECTOR Jeffrey Dever
DESIGNER Jeffrey Dever

5 DESIGN FIRM Dever Designs, Laurel, MD
CLIENT American Style Magazine
PROJECT American Crafts Abroad
ART DIRECTOR Jeffrey Dever
DESIGNER Jeffrey Dever
PHOTOGRAPHER Adrien Piron

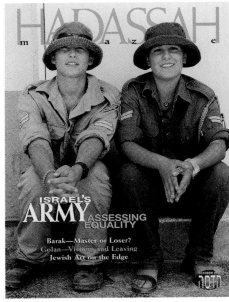

1

2

3

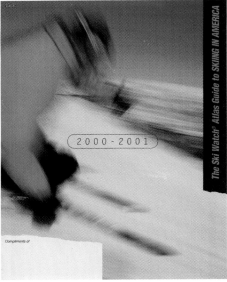

4

1 **DESIGN FIRM** Hadassah Magazine, New York, NY
PROJECT Overall Design October 2000
ART DIRECTOR Jodie Rossi
DESIGNER Jodie Rossi

2 **DESIGN FIRM** Jacqueline Barrett Design Inc., Oceanport, NJ
CLIENT National Association of Recording Merchandisers
PROJECT 2000-2001 Membership Directory
DESIGNER Jacqueline Barrett

3 **DESIGN FIRM** James Kuo, Forest Hills, NY
CLIENT New Immigrants Associates
PROJECT Freshman
ART DIRECTOR James Kuo
DESIGNER James Kuo
PHOTOGRAPHER James Kuo

4 **DESIGN FIRM** John Kallio Graphic Design, New Haven, CT
CLIENT CRN International
PROJECT Ski Watch Atlas
ART DIRECTOR John Kallio
DESIGNER John Kallio

5 **DESIGN FIRM** Jowaisas Design, Cazenovia, NY
CLIENT United Technologies Carrier Corp.
PROJECT Carrier World
DESIGNER Elizabeth Jowaisas

5

3

1 **DESIGN FIRM** MC2, East Greenbush, NY
CLIENT Minolta Corporation
PROJECT @ Minolta Magazine
ART DIRECTOR Leo Derkowski
DESIGNER Larry Ambrosino

2 **DESIGN FIRM** Messiah College, Grantham, PA
CLIENT Christians in the Visual Arts
PROJECT SEEN Journal
ART DIRECTOR Kathy T. Hettinga
DESIGNER Kathy T. Hettinga
EDITOR Barry Krammes
DESIGN ASSISTANT Jennifer Sheckels

3 **DESIGN FIRM** MLB Publisher, Chesapeake, VA
CLIENT Fort Monroe
PROJECT Dream World 2
ART DIRECTOR Melvin Beckett
DESIGNER Melvin Beckett

4 **DESIGN FIRM** Old Bergen Design, Jersey City, NJ
CLIENT Cahners
PROJECT Swatch Center 2000
ART DIRECTOR Kenneth Quail
DESIGNER Kenneth Quail
ILLUSTRATOR Kenneth Quail

5 **DESIGN FIRM** Orange County Register,
Santa Ana, CA
PROJECT Hawaii Live
ART DIRECTOR Kent Garrett
DESIGNERS Carol Rice, Anet Meyer

1

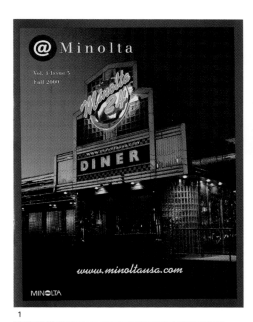

2

4

5

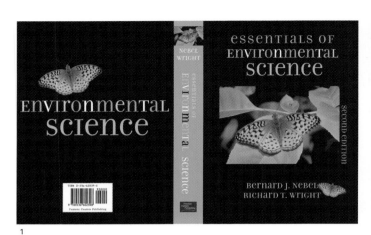

1

2

3

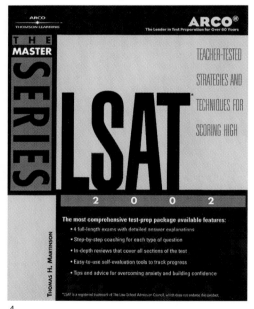

4

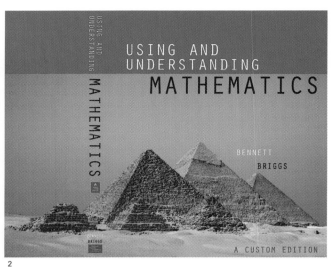

5

1 **DESIGN FIRM** Pearson Custom Publishing, Boston, MA
PROJECT Essentials of Environmental Science
ART DIRECTOR Kristen Kiley
DESIGNER Renee Sartell

2 **DESIGN FIRM** Pearson Custom Publishing, Boston, MA
PROJECT Using & Understanding Mathematics
ART DIRECTOR Kristen Kiley
DESIGNER Seamus Culligan

3 **DESIGN FIRM** Peterson's, Lawrenceville, NJ
PROJECT Private Secondary Schools 2002
ART DIRECTOR Allison Sullivan
DESIGNER Allison Sullivan

4 **DESIGN FIRM** Peterson's, Lawrenceville, NJ
PROJECT The Master Series LSAT 2002
ART DIRECTOR Allison Sullivan
DESIGNER Allison Sullivan

5 **DESIGN FIRM** Popular Mechanics, New York, NY
PROJECT Astronauts in Danger
ART DIRECTOR Bryan Canniff
ILLUSTRATOR Mark McCandlish

1

2

3

4

5

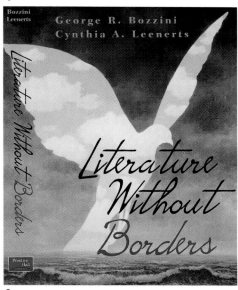

6

1 **DESIGN FIRM** Popular Mechanics, New York, NY
PROJECT A Century of Cars
ART DIRECTOR Bryan Canniff
PHOTOGRAPHER Ron Chapple

2 **DESIGN FIRM** Popular Mechanics, New York, NY
PROJECT 2001: A Car Odyssey
ART DIRECTOR Bryan Canniff

3 **DESIGN FIRM** Popular Mechanics, New York, NY
PROJECT Hotels in the Sky
ART DIRECTOR Bryan Canniff
ILLUSTRATOR Attila Hejja

4 **DESIGN FIRM** Popular Mechanics, New York, NY
PROJECT Deep and Deadly
ART DIRECTOR Bryan Canniff
ILLUSTRATOR Attila Hejja

5 **DESIGN FIRM** Popular Mechanics, New York, NY
PROJECT Making Connections
ART DIRECTOR Bryan Canniff
PHOTOGRAPHER Michel Tcherevkoff

6 **DESIGN FIRM** Prentice Hall, Higher Education, Upper Saddle River, NJ
CLIENT Carrie Brandon
PROJECT Literature Without Borders
ART DIRECTOR Robert Farrar-Wagner
DESIGNER Robert Farrar-Wagner

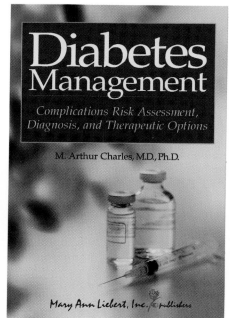

1

3

2

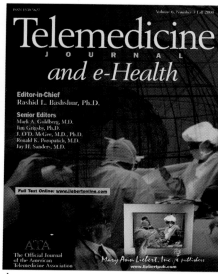

4

5

6

1 **DESIGN FIRM** RMS, Newark, CA
PROJECT Exposure Cover
ART DIRECTOR Yaping Xie
DESIGNER Yaping Xie
ILLUSTRATOR Yaping Xie

2 **DESIGN FIRM** SBN Magazine, Cleveland, OH
CLIENT SBN Magazine
PROJECT The Art of the Start-Up
ART DIRECTOR Beth A. Mihalek
DESIGNER Beth A. Mihalek
PHOTOGRAPHER Jim Jones
ILLUSTRATOR Beth A. Mihalek

3 **DESIGN FIRM** The Harquin Group, Pelham, NY
CLIENT Mary Ann Liebert Publishers
PROJECT Diabetes Management Journal Cover
ART DIRECTOR Sherry Bruck
ARTIST Eric Fjelde

4 **DESIGN FIRM** The Harquin Group, Pelham, NY
CLIENT Mary Ann Liebert Publishers
PROJECT Telemedicine and e-Health Journal Cover
ART DIRECTOR Sherry Bruck
ARTIST James Lambo

5 **DESIGN FIRM** The Humane Society of the United States,
Gaithersburg, MD
PROJECT 2000 Report of the President
ART DIRECTOR Paula Jaworski
DESIGNER Paula Jaworski
PHOTOGRAPHER Diane Ensign

6 **DESIGN FIRM** Zamboo, Marina Del Rey, CA
CLIENT Cox, Castle & Nicholson
PROJECT Forward Magazine
DESIGNERS Dave Zambotti, Becca Bootes
PHOTOGRAPHER David Zaitz

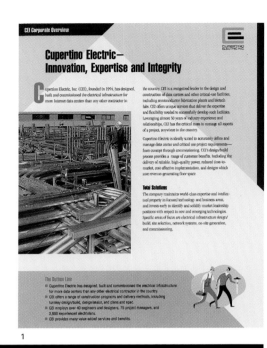

1

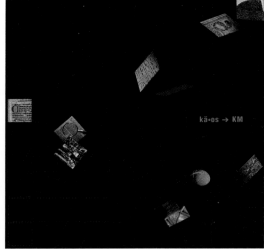

2

3

1 **DESIGN FIRM** Ann Hill Communications, San Rafael, CA
CLIENT Cupertino Electric, Inc.
PROJECT Brochure
ART DIRECTOR Jack Zoog
DESIGNER Jack Zoog
ILLUSTRATOR Ron Chan

2 **DESIGN FIRM** Artisa LLC, Plainsboro, NJ
CLIENT Ernst & Young
PROJECT ka.os KM (Knowledge Management Survey)
ART DIRECTOR Isabella D. Palowitch
DESIGNER Isabella D. Palowitch
PHOTOGRAPHER Richard Speedy, R&S Studio
ILLUSTRATOR Isabella D. Palowitch

3 **DESIGN FIRM** Belyea, Seattle, WA
PROJECT 12th Anniversary T-Shirt
ART DIRECTOR Patricia Belyea
DESIGNER Ron Lars Hansen

4 **DESIGN FIRM** Belyea, Seattle, WA
CLIENT ColorGraphics - Seattle
PROJECT Super 8 Brochure
ART DIRECTOR Patricia Belyea
DESIGNER Ron Lars Hansen
PHOTOGRAPHER Don Taylor

5 **DESIGN FIRM** Belyea, Seattle, WA
CLIENT Weyerhaeuser
PROJECT Containerboard Marketing-Asia
ART DIRECTOR Patricia Belyea
DESIGNER Ron Lars Hansen
ILLUSTRATOR Ning Yeh

4

5

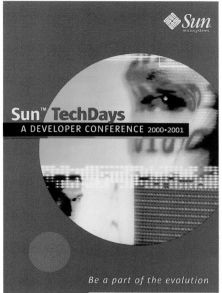

1

2

3

4

It's in your sights

5

1 **DESIGN FIRM** BI, Minneapolis, MN
   CLIENT Sun Microsystems
   PROJECT Sun Tech Days Campaign
   ART DIRECTOR Mark Geis
   DESIGNER Mark Geis

2 **DESIGN FIRM** BI, Minneapolis, MN
   CLIENT AC Nielsen
   PROJECT Recognition/Reward
   CREATIVE DIRECTOR Connie Schwader
   DESIGNER Melissa Lopez-Worm

3 **DESIGN FIRM** BI, Minneapolis, MN
   CLIENT Southern California Edison
   PROJECT Open Enrollment 2001 A Benefits Odyssey
   ART DIRECTOR Stephen Cook
   CREATIVE DIRECTOR Mary Rita Bottone

4 **DESIGN FIRM** BI, Minneapolis, MN
   CLIENT Toyota
   PROJECT Signature-TCEI
   ART DIRECTOR John Eastman
   CREATIVE DIRECTOR Julie Kline

5 **DESIGN FIRM** BI, Minneapolis, MN
   CLIENT Sprint PCS
   PROJECT It's in Your Sights
   ART DIRECTOR Mark Geis
   DESIGNER Mark Geis

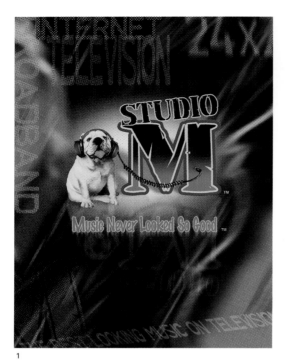

1

3

2

1 **DESIGN FIRM** Bob Wynne Studio, Woodland Hills, CA
CLIENT Studio M
PROJECT Brochure
ART DIRECTOR Bob Wynne
DESIGNER Bob Wynne

2 **DESIGN FIRM** Boston University, Boston, MA
PROJECT Hillel Brochure
ART DIRECTOR Wendy Garbarino
DESIGNER Wendy Garbarino
PHOTOGRAPHER BU Photo Services

3 **DESIGN FIRM** Brian J. Ganton & Associates, Cedar Grove, NJ
CLIENT Calico Cottage, Inc.
PROJECT Brochure
ART DIRECTOR Brian Ganton, Jr.
DESIGNER Mark Ganton
PHOTOGRAPHER Christopher Ganton
COPYWRITER Brian Ganton, Sr.

4 **DESIGN FIRM** Brown & Company Design, Portsmouth, NH
CLIENT Flywire
PROJECT Brochure
ART DIRECTOR David Markovsky
DESIGNERS Kelly Morin, Chris Lamy
PHOTOGRAPHER David Mendelson

5 **DESIGN FIRM** Campus Media Team-Campus Crusade for Christ, Orlando, FL
PROJECT Summer Projects Brochure
ART DIRECTOR Brian L. Byers
DESIGNER Brian L. Byers
PHOTOGRAPHERS Various Staff & Students

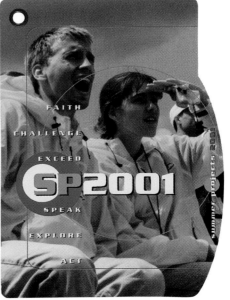

5

4

1

2

4

3

5

1 **DESIGN FIRM** Canon U.S.A., Lake Success, NY
PROJECT Presidents Club
DESIGNER Steve Okon

2 **DESIGN FIRM** Champagne/Lafayette Communications Inc., Natick, MA
CLIENT Josiah Guild & Sons
PROJECT Brochure
ART DIRECTOR Linda Luiso
DESIGNER Linda Luiso
PHOTOGRAPHER Bob Nash Studio

3 **DESIGN FIRM** Chebacco Design & Communications, LLC, Hamilton, MA
CLIENT Pohly & Partners
PROJECT Capabilities Brochure
ART DIRECTOR Chuck Carey
DESIGNERS Chuck Carey, Evan Sanderson

4 **DESIGN FIRM** Chona Designs, Atlanta, GA
CLIENT Craftforce
PROJECT Recruiting Brochure
ART DIRECTOR Chona Suva Dominguez
DESIGNER Chona Suva Dominguez
PHOTOGRAPHERS Various

5 **DESIGN FIRM** Clementi Associates, Hudson, MA
CLIENT Genrad
PROJECT Press Kit Folder
ART DIRECTOR William Glauner
DESIGNER William Glauner

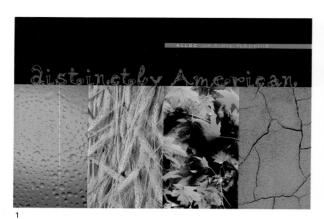

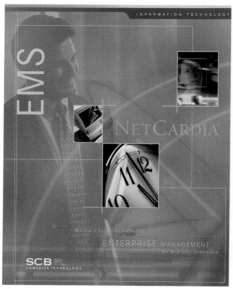

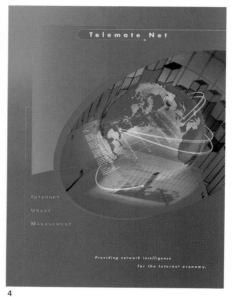

1 **DESIGN FIRM** Cramer-Krasselt, Milwaukee, WI
CLIENT Alloc Inc.
PROJECT Distinctly American
DESIGNER Shiere M. Melin
PHOTOGRAPHER Karen Melvin
ILLUSTRATOR Tom Siebers

2 **DESIGN FIRM** Cramer-Krasselt, Milwaukee, WI
CLIENT Appleton Papers Inc.
PROJECT Transformation
DESIGNER Shiere M. Melin

3 **DESIGN FIRM** Crawford/Mikus Design, Inc., Atlanta, GA
CLIENT SCB Computer Technologies
PROJECT Corporate Overview
ART DIRECTOR Elizabeth Crawford
DESIGNER Elizabeth Crawford

4 **DESIGN FIRM** Crawford/Mikus Design, Inc., Atlanta, GA
CLIENT Telemate.Net
PROJECT Corporate Brochure
ART DIRECTOR Elizabeth Crawford
DESIGNERS Elizabeth Crawford, Vicki Tagliatela
PHOTOGRAPHER John Grover

5 **DESIGN FIRM** Crawford/Mikus Design, Inc., Atlanta, GA
CLIENT McKessonHBOC ITB
PROJECT Corporate Product Brochure
ART DIRECTOR Elizabeth Crawford
DESIGNERS Michelle May, Elizabeth Crawford, Vicki Tagliatela

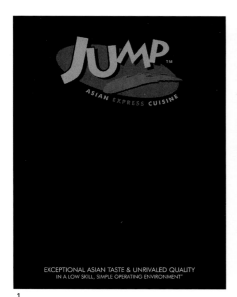

1

2

3

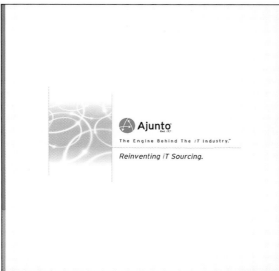

4

5

1 **DESIGN FIRM** Creative Design Solutions, Columbus, OH
CLIENT Jump International
PROJECT Marketing Package
ART DIRECTOR Chris Schweitzer
DESIGNER Chris Schweitzer
PHOTOGRAPHER Laura Sifferlin

2 **DESIGN FIRM** Creative Dynamics, Inc., Las Vegas, NV
CLIENT Capital Investment Company
PROJECT Fund Brochure Series
ART DIRECTORS Victor Rodriguez, Eddie Roberts
DESIGNERS Chris Smith, Victor Rodriguez

3 **DESIGN FIRM** Creative Services, Madison, CT
CLIENT CUNO Water Group
PROJECT Water, Life's Essential Ingredient
ART DIRECTOR Kim Barker Craven
DESIGNER Ellen Wagner
PHOTOGRAPHER Edwina Stevenson

4 **DESIGN FIRM** D4 Creative Group, Philadelphia, PA
CLIENT Ajunto
PROJECT Image Brochure
ART DIRECTOR Wicky Lee

5 **DESIGN FIRM** Dart Design, Fairfield, CT
CLIENT Savin
PROJECT Demo Pieces
ART DIRECTOR David Anderson
DESIGNER Kimberly Czar

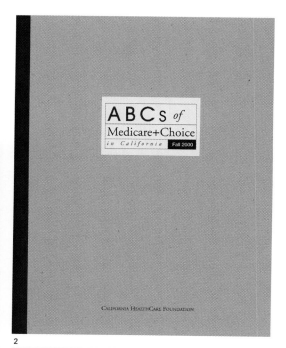

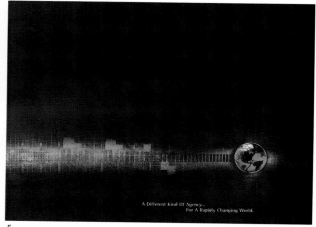

1 **DESIGN FIRM** Dawn Design, Chicago, IL
CLIENT Archer/American Wire
PROJECT Brochure
ART DIRECTOR Dawn Peccatiello
DESIGNER Dawn Peccatiello
PHOTOGRAPHER Dan Machnik

2 **DESIGN FIRM** Dennis Johnson Design, Oakland, CA
CLIENT California Healthcare Foundation
PROJECT ABCs of Medicare & Choice in California
ART DIRECTOR Dennis Johnson
DESIGNER Dennis Johnson
PHOTOGRAPHER Steve Fisch

3 **DESIGN FIRM** Design Matters Inc!, New York, NY
CLIENT Nuveen Investments
PROJECT Legg Mason POP2
ART DIRECTOR Stephen McAllister
DESIGNER Stephen McAllister

4 **DESIGN FIRM** Design Matters Inc!, New York, NY
CLIENT Nuveen Investments
PROJECT NDP Secondary Market
ART DIRECTOR Stephen McAllister
DESIGNER Stephen McAllister

5 **DESIGN FIRM** Designed Solutions, Kettering, OH
CLIENT The Berry Network
PROJECT Brochure
ART DIRECTOR Roxann Patrick
DESIGNER Joe Johnson

2

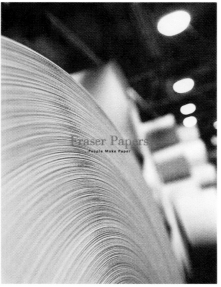

1

3

modus
Fraser Papers

Passport

8

4

Fraser Papers
People Make Paper

5

1 **DESIGN FIRM** DesignWorks NY, LLC, New York, NY
CLIENT SACO SmartVision
PROJECT Sales Brochure
DESIGNER Krista DeRuvo
ILLUSTRATOR Krista DeRuvo

2 **DESIGN FIRM** Di Vincenzo Design, Dobbs Ferry, NY
CLIENT CertCo
PROJECT RMX
ART DIRECTOR Dennis Di Vincenzo
DESIGNER Dennis Di Vincenzo
ILLUSTRATOR Dennis Di Vincenzo

3 **DESIGN FIRM** DiSanto Design, Wayne, PA
CLIENT Numeric Investors
PROJECT Capabilities Brochure
DESIGNER Rose DiSanto
PHOTOGRAPHER Bill Gallery

4 **DESIGN FIRM** Douglas Joseph Partners, Los Angeles, CA
CLIENT Fraser Papers
PROJECT Modus Series
ART DIRECTORS Douglas Joseph, Scott Lambert
DESIGNER Scott Lambert
PHOTOGRAPHERS Dave Teel, Jeff Zaruba, Eric Tucker,
Scott Lambert, Diane Koenigsberg, Rick Chou
ILLUSTRATORS Juliette Borda, Eddie Guy

5 **DESIGN FIRM** Douglas Joseph Partners, Los Angeles, CA
CLIENT Fraser Papers
PROJECT Corporate Brochure
ART DIRECTORS Douglas Joseph, Scott Lambert
DESIGNER Scott Lambert
PHOTOGRAPHER Chris Shinn

1 **DESIGN FIRM** Egads, Cranbury, NJ
CLIENT Robert Wood Johnson Medical School
PROJECT 2000 View Book
ART DIRECTOR Bruce Hanson
DESIGNER Bruce Hanson
PHOTOGRAPHER Dennis Connors

2 **DESIGN FIRM** Emily Rich Design,
Santa Monica, CA
CLIENT Shomrei Torah Synagogue
PROJECT A Spiritual Odyssey
ART DIRECTOR Emily Rich
DESIGNER Emily Rich
ILLUSTRATOR Emily Rich

3 **DESIGN FIRM** Fairly Painless Advertising,
Holland, MI
CLIENT Herman Miller
PROJECT Hanging Out Brochure
CREATIVE DIRECTOR, COPY Peter Bell
DESIGNERS Jason Alger, Rick Vanderleek

4 **DESIGN FIRM** Fisher Mears Associates,
Liberty, NY
CLIENT Woodstone Development Corp
PROJECT Wishes Brochure
DESIGNERS Anne Dubrovsky, Elise Mears

5 **DESIGN FIRM** Franklin Design Group,
Addison, TX
CLIENT University of North Texas -
EMBA Program
PROJECT Brochure
ART DIRECTOR Wendy Hanson
DESIGNERS Wendy Hanson, Amy Migliore
PHOTOGRAPHER Darrell Wilke

Herman Miller supports a family of four.

Goetz Sofa

One potato, two potato, three potato, four. Mark Goetz has designed the perfect place for today's nuclear family to veg out for a while.

3

4

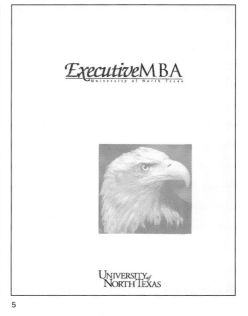

5

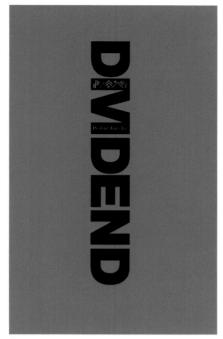

2

1

3

1 **DESIGN FIRM** frog design, Sunnyvale, CA
CLIENT Digital Island
PROJECT Corporate Identity and Collateral
ART DIRECTORS Gregory Hom, Eunice Ockerman
DESIGNERS Sarah Brolin, Roger Siu, Paul Obleas, Matt Roblee

2 **DESIGN FIRM** Gauger & Silva Associates, San Francisco, CA
CLIENT Dividend Homes
PROJECT Outlook Heights Brochure
ART DIRECTOR Bob Ankers

3 **DESIGN FIRM** Gauger & Silva Associates, San Francisco, CA
CLIENT Dividend Homes
PROJECT Corporate Brochure
ART DIRECTOR Bob Ankers
PHOTOGRAPHER John Horvers
ILLUSTRATOR Bob Ankers

4 **DESIGN FIRM** Gee & Chung Design, San Francisco, CA
CLIENT ComVentures
PROJECT Brochure
ART DIRECTORS Earl Gee, Fani Chung
DESIGNERS Earl Gee, Fani Chung, Kay Wu
PHOTOGRAPHER Henrik Kam

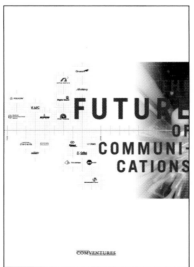

4A

4B

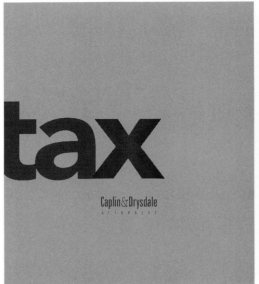

1

2

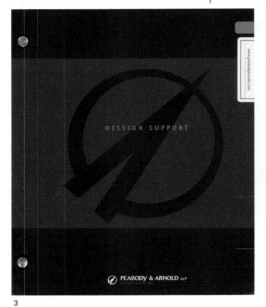

3

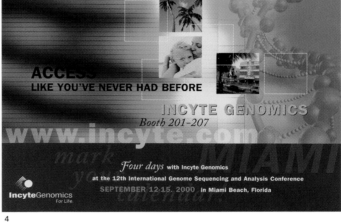

4

5

1 **DESIGN FIRM** Greenfield/Belser Ltd., Washington, DC
CLIENT Caplin & Drysdale
PROJECT Firm Brochure
ART DIRECTOR Burkey Belser
DESIGNER Gloria Gullikson
COPYWRITER Lise Anne Schwartz

2 **DESIGN FIRM** Greenfield/Belser Ltd., Washington, DC
CLIENT Blue Chair Design
PROJECT Firm Brochure
ART DIRECTOR Burkey Belser
DESIGNER Stephanie Fernandez
COPYWRITER Lise Anne Schwartz
ILLUSTRATOR Tom Cauler

3 **DESIGN FIRM** Greenfield/Belser Ltd., Washington, DC
CLIENT Peabody & Arnold
PROJECT Flex Brochure
ART DIRECTOR Burkey Belser
DESIGNER Tom Cameron
COPYWRITER Lise Anne Schwartz

4 **DESIGN FIRM** Group C Design, St. Louis, MO
CLIENT Incyte Genomics
PROJECT Tradeshow Collateral
ART DIRECTOR Ria Sharon
DESIGNERS Molly Alspaugh, Lois Arnold, Billie Knipfer, Lenore McClintock

5 **DESIGN FIRM** Group C Design, St. Louis, MO
CLIENT Broadwing Communications
PROJECT Collateral Material
ART DIRECTOR Ria Sharon
DESIGNER Billie Knipfer

1

2

3

4

5

1 **DESIGN FIRM** Gumption Design, New York, NY
CLIENT otec.com
PROJECT Sales Kit
ART DIRECTOR Evelyn Lontok
DESIGNER Evelyn Lontok

2 **DESIGN FIRM** Gunnar Swanson Design Office, Ventura, CA
CLIENT California Lutheran University Multimedia Program
PROJECT Brochure
ART DIRECTOR Gunnar Swanson
DESIGNER Gunnar Swanson
PHOTOGRAPHER Gunnar Swanson

3 **DESIGN FIRM** Harman Consumer Group, Woodbury, NY
CLIENT harman/kardon
PROJECT Consumer Literature
ART DIRECTORS Mike Keeley, Bob Abbatecola
DESIGNER Chris Rugen
PHOTOGRAPHER Josh McClure

4 **DESIGN FIRM** Harman Consumer Group, Woodbury, NY
CLIENT Infinity Systems
PROJECT Infinity Quotes and Accolades Brochure
ART DIRECTOR Bob Abbatecola
DESIGNER Chris Rugen
PHOTOGRAPHER Josh McClure

5 **DESIGN FIRM** Harman Consumer Group, Woodbury, NY
CLIENT JBL Car Audio
PROJECT JBL GTi Subwoofer Brochure
ART DIRECTOR John Cianti
DESIGNER Robin Witt
PHOTOGRAPHER Josh McClure

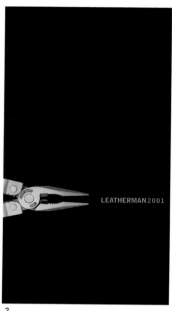

1

2

3

4

5

1 **DESIGN FIRM** Harper & Harper, New Haven, CT
CLIENT Blue Shamrock
PROJECT Leadership Training Brochures
ART DIRECTOR Barb Harper
DESIGNER IM Design

2 **DESIGN FIRM** Hornall Anderson Design Works, Inc., Seattle, WA
CLIENT Leatherman Tool Group
PROJECT Brand Brochure
ART DIRECTORS Jack Anderson, Katha Dalton
DESIGNERS Katha Dalton, Belinda Bowling, Gretchen Cook, Andrew Smith
PHOTOGRAPHER Ted Grudowski
ILLUSTRATOR Ted Grudowski

3 **DESIGN FIRM** Hornall Anderson Design Works, Inc., Seattle, WA
CLIENT Aerzone
PROJECT Brochures
ART DIRECTOR Mark Popich
DESIGNERS Mark Popich, Mary McCafferty, Ed Lee, Gretchen Cook, Andrew Smith

4 **DESIGN FIRM** Hornall Anderson Design Works, Inc., Seattle, WA
CLIENT Heavenly Stone
PROJECT Promotional Rock
ART DIRECTOR Jack Anderson
DESIGNERS Jack Anderson, Henry Yiu
CALLIGRAPHY Taka Suzuki

5 **DESIGN FIRM** Howard Belk/Red Sky, New York, NY
CLIENT Appleton Coated LLC
PROJECT Rayman-Manray
ART DIRECTOR Howard Belk
DESIGNER Red Sky
PHOTOGRAPHER Victor John Penner Photography

1

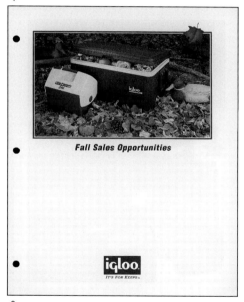

2

3

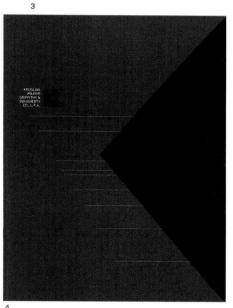

4

5

1 **DESIGN FIRM** Howell Design, Inc., Williamsburg, VA
CLIENT Basofil Heat and Flame Resistant Fiber
PROJECT Capabilities Brochure
ART DIRECTOR Kathy Howell
DESIGNER Ben Griffon
PHOTOGRAPHERS Bill Boxer Photography,
Dave Fornell, N.C. State University

2 **DESIGN FIRM** Igloo Products, Houston, TX
PROJECT Fall Sales Opportunities Sell Sheet
ART DIRECTOR Bill Biles
DESIGNER Bill Biles
PHOTOGRAPHER Joe Abraham

3 **DESIGN FIRM** Ilium Associates, Inc., Bellevue, WA
CLIENT Trammell Crow Residential
PROJECT Alexan CityPlace Leasing Brochure
ART DIRECTOR Don Sellars
DESIGNER Angela Hopkins

4 **DESIGN FIRM** Innis Maggiore Group, Canton, OH
CLIENT Krugliak Wilkins
PROJECT Future of Law Brochure
ART DIRECTOR Jeff Monter
DESIGNER Jennifer Bamby
PHOTOGRAPHER Joe Smithberger

5 **DESIGN FIRM** J. Paul Getty Trust-Publications Services,
Los Angeles, CA
CLIENT Getty Research Institute
PROJECT Mexico Exhibition Brochure
DESIGNER Silvina Nieponmiszcze

1

2

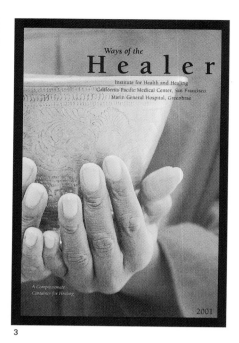

3

4

5

1 **DESIGN FIRM** Jensen Design Associates,
Long Beach, CA
CLIENT Canon Computers Systems Inc.
PROJECT Take One Brochures
ART DIRECTOR David Jensen
DESIGNERS Virginia Teager, Alyssa Igawa

2 **DESIGN FIRM** Jostens Creative, Bloomington, MN
CLIENT Martin Marietta Materials
PROJECT Making the Grade
ART DIRECTOR Ginger Flemming
DESIGNER Ginger Flemming
PHOTOGRAPHER Heidi Ehaldt
ILLUSTRATOR George Rysavy

3 **DESIGN FIRM** Julie Chun Design, Mill Valley, CA
CLIENT California Pacific Medical Center -
Institute for Health & Healing
PROJECT Ways of the Healer Journal
ART DIRECTOR Julie L. Chun
DESIGNER Julie L. Chun
PHOTOGRAPHER Penny Bauer

4 **DESIGN FIRM** Kelley Communications Group,
Dublin, OH
CLIENT Lucent Technologies
PROJECT Catalyst Flip Side
ART DIRECTOR Kevin Ronnebaum
DESIGNER Beth Czekalski
PHOTOGRAPHER Stephen Webster

5 **DESIGN FIRM** Kircher, Washington, DC
CLIENT American Chemical Society
PROJECT ProSpectives Program
ART DIRECTORS Bruce E. Morgan, John Frantz
DESIGNERS Bruce E. Morgan, John Frantz

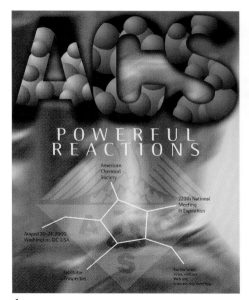

1

2

3

4

5

1 **DESIGN FIRM** Kircher, Washington, DC
CLIENT American Chemical Society
PROJECT 220th National Exposition Brochure
ART DIRECTOR Bruce E. Morgan
DESIGNER Bruce E. Morgan

2 **DESIGN FIRM** Kircher, Washington, DC
CLIENT Direct Marketing Association
PROJECT The DMA 84th Annual Prospectus
ART DIRECTOR Dorothy Rudzik
DESIGNER Dorothy Rudzik

3 **DESIGN FIRM** Kirshenbaum Communications,
San Francisco, CA
CLIENT Prophet
PROJECT Presentation Folder & Inserts
ART DIRECTOR Jim Neczypor
DESIGNER Jim Neczypor

4 **DESIGN FIRM** Leimer Cross Design, Seattle, WA
CLIENT Monadnock Paper Mills
PROJECT This Piece is About Just One Annual Report
ART DIRECTOR Kerry Leimer
DESIGNER Kerry Leimer
PHOTOGRAPHER Jeff Corwin

5 **DESIGN FIRM** March of Dimes, White Plains, NY
PROJECT Celebrity Recruitment Brochure
ART DIRECTORS Barbara Jones, Marsha Maurer
DESIGNER Michael Rae

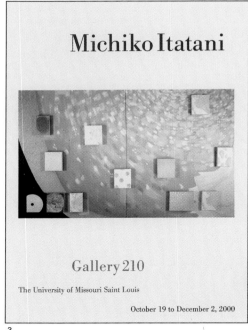

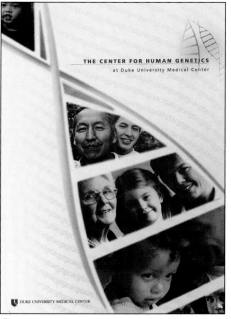

1 **DESIGN FIRM** Mark Selfe Design, Emeryville, CA
CLIENT Vectiv
PROJECT Brochure
ART DIRECTOR Mark Selfe
DESIGNERS Mark Selfe, Erin Delorefice

2 **DESIGN FIRM** McCulloch Design, Raleigh, NC
CLIENT IBM
PROJECT TechConnect Brochure
ART DIRECTOR Stephen McCulloch
DESIGNER Stephen McCulloch

3 **DESIGN FIRM** Michael Fanizza Designs, Haslett, MI
CLIENT Gallery 210, University of Missouri Saint Louis
PROJECT Michiko Itatani Brochure
ART DIRECTOR Michael Fanizza
DESIGNER Michael Fanizza

4 **DESIGN FIRM** Miriello Grafico, Inc., San Diego, CA
CLIENT Creative Spa
PROJECT Spa Manicure Brochure
ART DIRECTOR Dennis Garcia
DESIGNER Dennis Garcia

5 **DESIGN FIRM** Mission House Creative, Raleigh, NC
CLIENT Duke Medical Center
PROJECT The Center for Human Genetics Brochure
ART DIRECTOR Carol Roessner
DESIGNER Carol Roessner
ILLUSTRATOR Carol Roessner

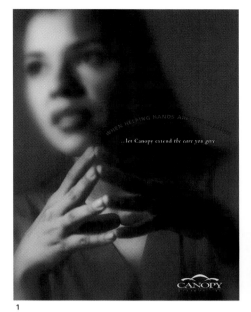

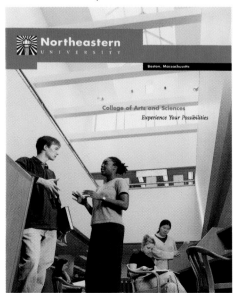

1

2

3

4

5

1 **DESIGN FIRM** Mission House Creative, Raleigh, NC
CLIENT Canopy Systems, Inc.
PROJECT Sales Package
ART DIRECTOR Carol Roessner
DESIGNERS Carol Roessner, Tamara Timmons
ILLUSTRATOR Carol Roessner

2 **DESIGN FIRM** Natalie Kitamura Design, San Francisco, CA
CLIENT Cal Fed Banking
PROJECT Welcome Kit
ART DIRECTOR Natalie Kitamura
DESIGNERS Lisa Winter, Wesley Quock

3 **DESIGN FIRM** Nesnadny + Schwartz, Cleveland, OH
CLIENT SMART Papers
PROJECT Knightkote Big Brochure
ART DIRECTOR Joyce Nesnadny, Michelle Moehler
DESIGNER Michelle Moehler
PHOTOGRAPHERS Alex Ardenti Photography, Ron Stewart,
Raoul Gradvohl, Henry Horenstein, Design Photography, Inc.

4 **DESIGN FIRM** Northeastern University Publications, Boston, MA
CLIENT Office of Undergraduate Admissions
PROJECT Campus Guide
ART DIRECTOR Robert S. Davison
DESIGNER Robert S. Davison
ILLUSTRATOR David Merrill

5 **DESIGN FIRM** Northeastern University Publications, Boston, MA
CLIENT Office of Undergraduate Admissions
PROJECT College of Arts and Sciences Viewbook
ART DIRECTOR Robert S. Davison
DESIGNER Kelly Milligan
PHOTOGRAPHERS Tony Rinaldo, Tom Kates

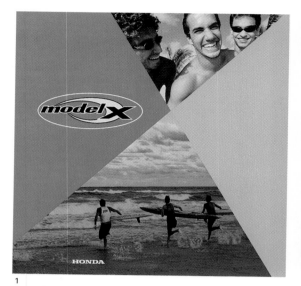

1

2

3

4

5

1 **DESIGN FIRM** Oakwood DC, Manhattan Beach, CA
   CLIENT American Honda
   PROJECT ModelX Concept Car Press Folder
   ART DIRECTOR Rick Delome
   DESIGNER Tony Pigram

2 **DESIGN FIRM** Olson, Kotowski & Co., Redondo Beach, CA
   CLIENT Epson America, Inc.
   PROJECT K-12 Education Guide
   ART DIRECTOR Janice Olson
   DESIGNER Paul Archer

3 **DESIGN FIRM** Olson, Kotowski & Co., Redondo Beach, CA
   CLIENT Epson America, Inc.
   PROJECT Photo Journal
   ART DIRECTOR Janice Olson
   DESIGNER Annette Steiner

4 **DESIGN FIRM** Philip Morris Management Corp., New York, NY
   PROJECT Working to Make a Difference
   ART DIRECTOR Walter Kryshak
   DESIGNER Walter Kryshak

5 **DESIGN FIRM** Phinney/Bischoff Design House, Seattle, WA
   CLIENT Seattle Public Library Foundation
   PROJECT Brochure
   ART DIRECTOR Leslie Phinney
   DESIGNER Dean Hart
   ILLUSTRATOR Dean Hart

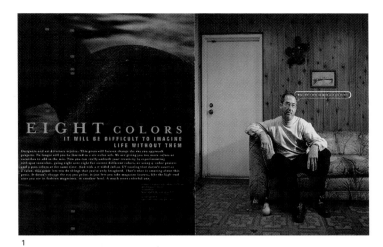

1

2

3

1 **DESIGN FIRM** Pinkhaus, Miami, FL
  CLIENT George Rice & Sons
  PROJECT Promotional Brochure
  ART DIRECTORS John Choe, Todd Houser
  DESIGNERS Todd Houser, Raelene Mercer
  PHOTOGRAPHER Michael Thoennes
  COPYWRITER Frank Cunningham
  PRODUCTION Suzanne Bernstein

2 **DESIGN FIRM** PrimeLook Inc., New York, NY
  CLIENT Travelers Life & Annuity
  PROJECT Sales Kits
  ART DIRECTOR PrimeLook Inc.
  DESIGNER PrimeLook Inc.

3 **DESIGN FIRM** PrimeLook Inc., New York, NY
  CLIENT New York Life
  PROJECT MainStay Annuities Branding
  ART DIRECTOR PrimeLook Inc.
  DESIGNER PrimeLook Inc.

4 **DESIGN FIRM** PrimeLook Inc., New York, NY
  CLIENT Met Life
  PROJECT Event Planning Kit
  ART DIRECTOR PrimeLook Inc.
  DESIGNER PrimeLook Inc.

5 **DESIGN FIRM** Rock-Tenn Company, Norcross, GA
  CLIENT RTS Packaging Division
  PROJECT Brochure
  DESIGNER Greg Vaughn

4

5

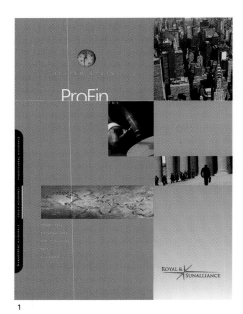

1 **DESIGN FIRM** Royal & SunAlliance, Charlotte, NC
CLIENT ProFin
PROJECT Marketing Kit
DESIGNER Harry Lambert

2 **DESIGN FIRM** Royal & SunAlliance, Charlotte, NC
CLIENT Green Shield
PROJECT Brochure
DESIGNER Jane Love
ILLUSTRATOR Jane Love

3 **DESIGN FIRM** Rule 29, Elgin, IL
CLIENT Kraft Foods, Inc.
PROJECT Over the Top III, Maui
ART DIRECTORS Justin Ahrens, Jim Boborci
DESIGNERS Justin Ahrens, Jim Boborci

4 **DESIGN FIRM** Rutgers, The State University of New Jersey, New Brunswick, NJ
CLIENT Graduate School of Management
PROJECT Rutgers MBA
ART DIRECTOR John Van Cleaf
DESIGNER John Van Cleaf

5 **DESIGN FIRM** Rutgers, The State University of New Jersey, New Brunswick, NJ
CLIENT Rutgers University
PROJECT Perspectives
ART DIRECTOR John Van Cleaf
DESIGNER John Van Cleaf
ILLUSTRATOR Lisa Henderling

1

2

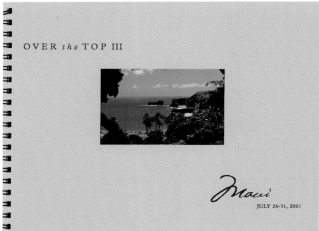

3

4

5

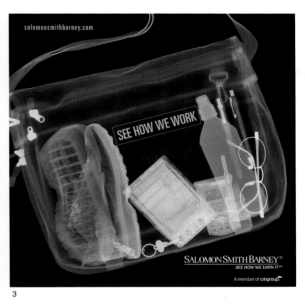

1 **DESIGN FIRM** Salomon Smith Barney, New York, NY
CLIENT Women & Co.
PROJECT Brochure
ART DIRECTOR Melita Sussman
DESIGNER Candice Stern
PROJECT MANAGER Christina Luongo

2 **DESIGN FIRM** Salomon Smith Barney, New York, NY
PROJECT Imagine No Limits
ART DIRECTOR Melita Sussman
DESIGNER Frank Gitro
PHOTOGRAPHER Earl Ripling
ILLUSTRATOR Project Manager Geri Brinker

3 **DESIGN FIRM** Salomon Smith Barney, New York, NY
PROJECT See How We Work
ART DIRECTORS Melita Sussman, Laurie Elvove
DESIGNER Laurie Elvove
PHOTOGRAPHER David Arky
PROJECT MANAGER Geri Brinker

4 **DESIGN FIRM** Salomon Smith Barney, New York, NY
CLIENT Robinson-Humphrey
PROJECT Recruitment Brochure
ART DIRECTOR Melita Sussman
DESIGNER Todd Sargood

5 **DESIGN FIRM** Salomon Smith Barney, New York, NY
PROJECT Private Wealth Management Brochure
ART DIRECTOR Melita Sussman
DESIGNER Todd Sargood

2

1 **DESIGN FIRM** Salomon Smith Barney, New York, NY
PROJECT Mutual Funds Folder
ART DIRECTOR Melita Sussman
DESIGNER Todd Sargood

2 **DESIGN FIRM** Salomon Smith Barney, New York, NY
PROJECT Firm Capabilities Folder
ART DIRECTOR Melita Sussman
DESIGNER Candice Stern
PHOTOGRAPHER Liana Miuccio
PROJECT MANAGER Geri Brinker

3 **DESIGN FIRM** SCK Design Inc., Cleveland, OH
CLIENT Case Western Reserve University Weatherhead Executive Education
PROJECT The Executive MBA Program
DESIGNER Steve Schultz

4 **DESIGN FIRM** Shea, Minneapolis, MN
CLIENT Dayton-Hudson's/Marshall Field's
PROJECT Hinky Dink's Menu
ART DIRECTOR Holly Utech
DESIGNER Holly Utech, Jason Wittwer

5 **DESIGN FIRM** Sherie Presta Creative Services, Chicago, IL
CLIENT 3PF
PROJECT Corrugated Capabilities Brochure & Slim Jim
ART DIRECTOR Sherie Presta
CREATIVE DIRECTOR Sherie Presta
COPYWRITER Julia Bailey
PHOTOGRAPHER John Frangoulis
ILLUSTRATOR John Virissimo

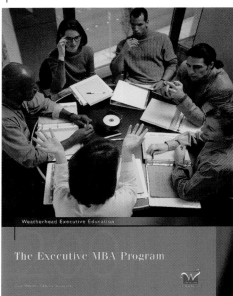

3

4

5

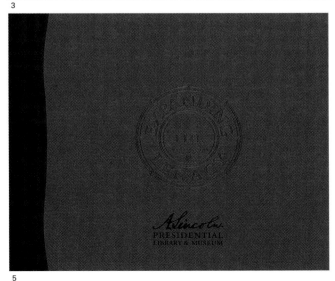

1

2

3

4

5

1 **DESIGN FIRM** Sherman Advertising, New York, NY
CLIENT Sterling Properties
PROJECT Sterling Green Brochure
ART DIRECTOR Sharon Elaine Lloyd
DESIGNER Sharon Elaine Lloyd
ILLUSTRATOR Robert Steele

2 **DESIGN FIRM** SilverSpur Creative Group, Inc., Norwalk, CT
CLIENT Phoenix Press, Inc.
PROJECT It's All About Relationships

3 **DESIGN FIRM** SJI Associates Inc., New York, NY
CLIENT Golden Books
PROJECT Nickelodeon Sales Kit
ART DIRECTOR Jill Vinitsky
DESIGNER Alex Rekasi

4 **DESIGN FIRM** Skidmore Inc., Southfield, MI
CLIENT Village Green Companies
PROJECT Fisher Building Brochure
ART DIRECTOR Mae Skidmore
DESIGNER Julie Pincus

5 **DESIGN FIRM** Stan Gellman Graphic Design, St. Louis, MO
CLIENT Abraham Lincoln Presidential Library and Museum Foundation
PROJECT Expanding the Legacy
ART DIRECTOR Barry Tilson
DESIGNER Mike Donovan

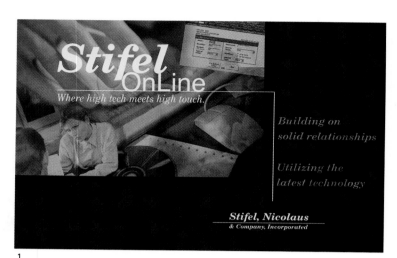

1

2

4

3

1   **DESIGN FIRM** Stifel, Nicolaus & Company, Inc., St. Louis, MO
    CLIENT Stifel, Nicolaus & Company, Inc.
    PROJECT Stifel OnLine Brochure
    ART DIRECTOR Lynda Hofstetter
    DESIGNER Melinda Samarco

2   **DESIGN FIRM** Stival Design, Port Washington, NY
    CLIENT TENS Machine Co., Inc.
    PROJECT Brochure
    ART DIRECTOR Gina Stival
    DESIGNER Gina Stival
    PHOTOGRAPHER Josh McClure, Island Color

3   **DESIGN FIRM** Stuart Bran Advertising, Allendale, NJ
    CLIENT The Braff Group
    PROJECT On Your Side Brochure
    ART DIRECTOR Stuart Bran
    DESIGNER Stuart Bran

4   **DESIGN FIRM** Studio North, North Chicago, IL
    CLIENT Visual Insights
    PROJECT Collateral Material
    ART DIRECTOR Mark Schneider
    DESIGNERS Erik Peterson, Jason Onken
    ILLUSTRATOR Steve Herberger

5   **DESIGN FIRM** Studio North, North Chicago, IL
    CLIENT BP
    PROJECT Recruitment Materials
    DESIGNER Jason Onken

5

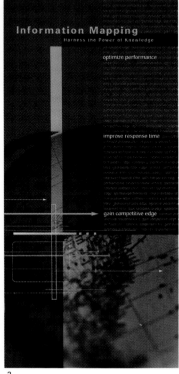

1

3

The Boston Globe Fundraising Program

4

Marathon 2001
The Globe's Coverage
of the Boston Marathon

The Boston Globe

5

2

1 **DESIGN FIRM** Studio North, North Chicago, IL
CLIENT Abbott Laboratories
PROJECT Recruitment Brochure
DESIGNER Misty Castaldi

2 **DESIGN FIRM** Sullivan Creative, Watertown, MA
CLIENT Information Mapping
PROJECT Brochure
ART DIRECTOR David Ferreira

3 **DESIGN FIRM** TGD Communications, Inc.,
Alexandria, VA
CLIENT National Academy of Engineering
PROJECT Awards Brochure
ART DIRECTOR Frank Pastorini
DESIGNER Frank Pastorini, Kati Becker
PHOTOGRAPHER Scott Braman

4 **DESIGN FIRM** The Boston Globe, Boston, MA
PROJECT Fundraising Brochure
ART DIRECTOR Lisa Sullo
DESIGNER Don Norton
ILLUSTRATOR Sean McNaughton

5 **DESIGN FIRM** The Boston Globe, Boston, MA
PROJECT 2000 Boston Marathon P.C.
ART DIRECTOR Steve Peña
DESIGNER Mike Togo

2

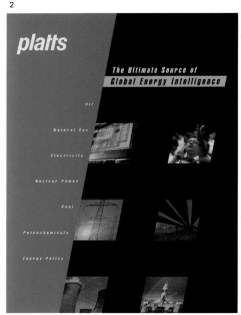

4

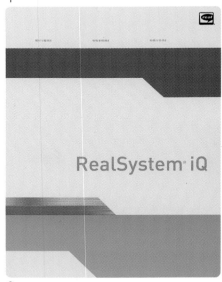

3

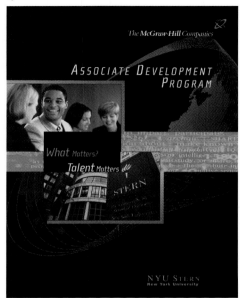

5

1 **DESIGN FIRM** The Boston Globe, Boston, MA
PROJECT Destination Florida P.C.
ART DIRECTOR Steve Peña
DESIGNER Mike Togo

2 **DESIGN FIRM** The Boston Globe, Boston, MA
PROJECT Spring Real Estate Review
ART DIRECTOR Lisa Sullo
DESIGNER Monique Walton

3 **DESIGN FIRM** The Leonhardt Group, Seattle, WA
CLIENT RealNetworks
PROJECT Media Systems Collateral
ART DIRECTOR Ray Ueno
DESIGNER Jason Gomez
ILLUSTRATOR Carlos Montalvan

4 **DESIGN FIRM** The McGraw-Hill Companies,
New York, NY
CLIENT Platts
PROJECT Global Energy Intelligence Brochure
ART DIRECTOR Marianne Johnston
CREATIVE DIRECTOR Paul Biedermann

5 **DESIGN FIRM** The McGraw-Hill Companies,
New York, NY
CLIENT Human Resources
PROJECT Associate Development Program
ART DIRECTOR Marianne Johnston
DESIGNER Bryan Dew
CREATIVE DIRECTOR Terrence Gaughan

1 **DESIGN FIRM** The McGraw-Hill Companies, New York, NY
CLIENT Architectural Record
PROJECT Media Kit
ART DIRECTOR Marianne Johnston
DESIGNER Bryan Dew
CREATIVE DIRECTOR Terrence Gaughan

2 **DESIGN FIRM** The Media Game®, Miami Beach, FL
CLIENT Business of Restaurants, Inc.
PROJECT Campaign-Brochure
ART DIRECTOR Christina Ricci
DESIGNER Christina Ricci
PHOTOGRAPHER Barbara Pittman

3 **DESIGN FIRM** The Rockbridge Group, Bethesda, MD
CLIENT M&R Strategic Services
PROJECT Brochure
ART DIRECTOR Bill Glover
DESIGNER Bill Glover

4 **DESIGN FIRM** The Seibels Bruce Group, Inc., Columbia, SC
CLIENT Insurance Network Services
PROJECT Sales Kit
ART DIRECTOR Amy C. Kulp
DESIGNER Amy C. Kulp

5 **DESIGN FIRM** Tieken Design & Creative Services, Phoenix, AZ
CLIENT Evolution.com
PROJECT Positioning Brochure
ART DIRECTOR Fred E. Tieken
DESIGNERS Fred E. Tieken, Stan Hattaway

1

3

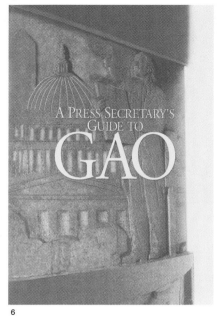

4

5

EVERYTHING
YOU NEED
IN
REAL ESTATE
&
HOME
COVERAGE.
PERIOD.

6

A PRESS SECRETARY'S
GUIDE TO
GAO

CLARENCE
PAGE

A liberal
with a
surprising
right hook

TOWSON
UNIVERSITY

Maryland, U.S.A.

1 **DESIGN FIRM** Tony Mistretta Graphics, Chicago, IL
CLIENT Aardvark Landscape & Masonry
PROJECT Brochure
ART DIRECTOR Amanda Rose Powell
DESIGNERS Tony Mistretta, Patrick Kelly

2 **DESIGN FIRM** Towson University, Towson, MD
CLIENT Towson University Alumni
PROJECT Homecoming Brochure
ART DIRECTOR Mike Dunne
DESIGNER Keith Matthews
ILLUSTRATOR Rick Guariglia

3 **DESIGN FIRM** Towson University, Towson, MD
PROJECT International Portfolio 2000-2001
ART DIRECTOR Rick Pallansch
DESIGNER Rick Pallansch
PHOTOGRAPHER Kanji Takeno

4 **DESIGN FIRM** Tribune Media Services, Chicago, IL
PROJECT Clarence Page Sell Sheet
ART DIRECTOR Susan V. Holton
DESIGNER Susan V. Holton
PHOTOGRAPHER Chuck Kennedy

5 **DESIGN FIRM** Tribune Media Services, Chicago, IL
PROJECT Real Estate Sales Folder
ART DIRECTOR Susan V. Holton
DESIGNER Stephani Bode Kuehn

6 **DESIGN FIRM** U.S. General Accounting Office, Washington, DC
CLIENT Public Affairs
PROJECT GAO Guides
ART DIRECTOR Theresa Mechem
DESIGNER Theresa Mechem
PHOTOGRAPHER Richard Rockburn

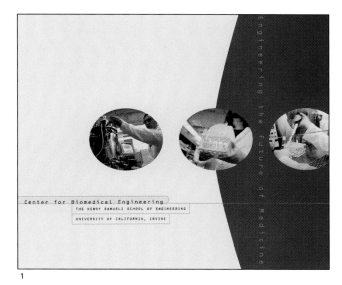

1

2

3

4

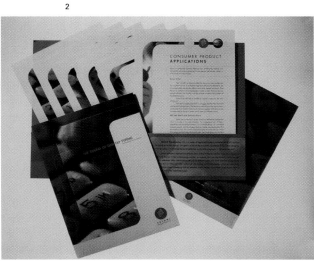

5

1 **DESIGN FIRM** Vince Rini Design, Huntington Beach, CA
CLIENT UC Irvine
PROJECT Biomedical Research Brochure
ART DIRECTOR Vince Rini
DESIGNER Vince Rini
PHOTOGRAPHER Stephen Swintek

2 **DESIGN FIRM** VPA, Santa Monica, CA
CLIENT Photobition USA
PROJECT Tio Case
CREATIVE DIRECTOR Vladimir Paperny
DESIGNER Vladimir Sonkin

3 **DESIGN FIRM** Wee Small Hours Design, New York, NY
CLIENT Eatoni Ergonomics
PROJECT Folder and Inserts
ART DIRECTOR Ellen Hibschweiler
DESIGNER Marianna Dutra

4 **DESIGN FIRM** Wee Small Hours Design, New York, NY
CLIENT Department of Orthopaedic Surgery at Columbia University
PROJECT Columbia University - Orthopaedics Brochure
ART DIRECTOR Ellen Hibschweiler
DESIGNERS Saehee Lee, Marianna Dutra, Rie Oshiro

5 **DESIGN FIRM** WESTAT Graphic Arts Department, Rockville, MD
PROJECT Clinical Trials
ART DIRECTOR Shayna Heller
DESIGNER Brian Henigin

1

2

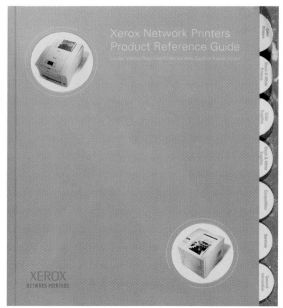

PRINTUTOPIA™

A GRAPHIC ARTS PUBLICATION FROM THE MAKERS OF UTOPIA®

A CASE STUDY ON PAPER AND PRINT
N° 1

ALTERED STATES

*Using Color Alterations
to Fuel Your Alter Ego*

3

PRINT™

A GRAPHIC ARTS PUBLICATION FROM THE MAKERS OF UTOPIA®

A CASE STUDY ON PAPER AND PRINT
N° 2

SHADES OF ONE

*Taking the Monotony Out of
Monochromatic Themes*

4

1 **DESIGN FIRM** Worldwide Meetings & Communications,
Silver Spring, MD
CLIENT Social and Scientific Systems
PROJECT Corporate Materials
ART DIRECTOR Beverly Valdez
DESIGNERS Paweena Pimkwan, Paul Ponton,
Laura Spofford

2 **DESIGN FIRM** Xerox Corporation, Wilsonville, OR
PROJECT Product Reference Guide
ART DIRECTOR Ami Danielson
DESIGNERS Ami Danielson, Patrick Prothe
COPYWRITER Ross Burdick

3 **DESIGN FIRM** Yelton Design, Sherwood, WI
CLIENT Appleton Coated LLC
PROJECT Altered States
DESIGNER Yelton Design

4 **DESIGN FIRM** Yelton Design, Sherwood, WI
CLIENT Appleton Coated LLC
PROJECT Shades of One
DESIGNER Yelton Design

5 **DESIGN FIRM** Zamboo, Marina Del Rey, CA
CLIENT eIndia.com
PROJECT Corporate Brochure
ART DIRECTOR Dave Zambotti
DESIGNER Jeff Allison

6 **DESIGN FIRM** Zermatt, Luling, LA
CLIENT Fat Tuesday
PROJECT Find Yourself in a Daiquiri
ART DIRECTOR Matt Touchard
DESIGNERS Matt Touchard, Heather White
PHOTOGRAPHER Ron Calamia

5

6

01·01·00

july

"To see a world in a grain
of sand, and a heaven in
a wildflower, hold infinity
in the palm of your hand
and eternity in an hour."

William Blake

1

COMMITMENT

Promises That Are KEPT

OCTOBER

2

3

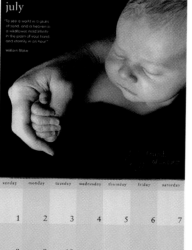

july

4

5

1 **DESIGN FIRM** Agnew Moyer Smith, Inc., Pittsburgh, PA
   CLIENT Quantapoint, Inc.
   PROJECT 2001 Calendar
   COPYWRITER Melissa Kelley
   DESIGNER Randy Ziegler
   PRODUCTION Mike Duda
   ILLUSTRATOR Kurt Hess

2 **DESIGN FIRM** Capital Associated Industries, Raleigh, NC
   CLIENT Key Risk Management
   PROJECT 2001 Calendar
   ART DIRECTOR Stephen McCulloch
   DESIGNER Stephen McCulloch

3 **DESIGN FIRM** Company X, Summit, NJ
   CLIENT Shire US Inc.
   PROJECT Carbatrol Epilepsy Calendar
   ART DIRECTOR Thomas Sacco
   CREATIVE DIRECTORS Laura Warburton, Carol Hill
   COPYWRITER Richard Sullivan

4 **DESIGN FIRM** Gorman Richardson Architects, Hopkinton, MA
   PROJECT Quarterly Mailing Calendar Cards
   DESIGNERS Doug Hill, Lesley Breen
   PHOTOGRAPHERS John Horner, Anton Grassel
   ILLUSTRATORS Doug Hill, Lesley Breen

5 **DESIGN FIRM** March of Dimes, White Plains, NY
   PROJECT Calendar 2001
   ART DIRECTORS Barbara Jones, Sharon Mahoney
   DESIGNER William Masto
   PHOTOGRAPHER Jennifer Coate

2

1

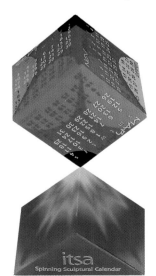

4

3

5

1 **DESIGN FIRM** Natalie Kitamura Design, San Francisco, CA
PROJECT Self Promotion Calendar/Gift Wrap
ART DIRECTOR Natalie Kitamura
DESIGNERS Elizabeth Hedan, Lisa Winter
ILLUSTRATORS Elizabeth Hedan, Lisa Winter

2 **DESIGN FIRM** Olver Dunlop Associates, Chicago, IL
CLIENT Marlena Agency
PROJECT 2001 American Indian Myths and Legends
ART DIRECTOR Kara Kuster
DESIGNER Kara Kuster
ILLUSTRATOR Marlena Agency

3 **DESIGN FIRM** Page Design, Inc., Sacramento, CA
CLIENT Powerschool Inc.
PROJECT Calendar
ART DIRECTORS Paul Page, Chris Brown
DESIGNERS Chris Brown, Sherril Cortez
ILLUSTRATOR Chris Brown

4 **DESIGN FIRM** Page Design, Inc., Sacramento, CA
CLIENT Gene Berthelsen-Caltrans
PROJECT 2001 Calendar - Strategic Performance
ART DIRECTORS Paul Page, Tracy Titus
DESIGNERS Ryan Holcomb, Sherril Cortez
PHOTOGRAPHER Caltrans Photo Lab

5 **DESIGN FIRM** Para Designers Inc., Woodstock, IL
PROJECT ITSA Spinning Sculptural Calendar 2000 and 2001
ART DIRECTOR Eric Neumann
DESIGNER Mari Baskin
ILLUSTRATOR Eric Neumann

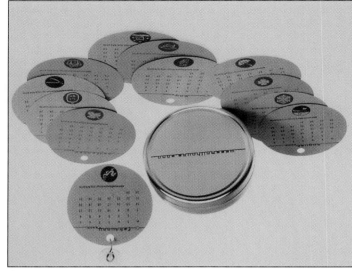

4

1

5

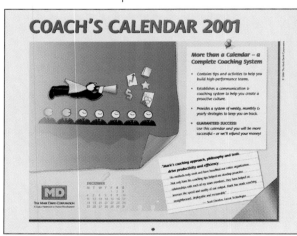

2

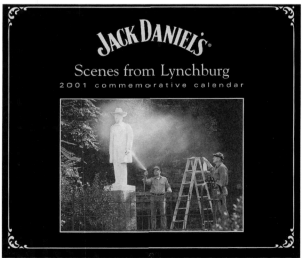

3

1 **DESIGN FIRM** Pinkhaus, Miami, FL
  CLIENT Rene Farrait/Miguel Cancel
  PROJECT Calendar
  ART DIRECTOR Carlos Perez
  DESIGNER Carlos Perez
  PHOTOGRAPHER Blasius Erlinger
  CREATIVE DIRECTOR Tim Meraz

2 **DESIGN FIRM** The Mark David Corporation, San Mateo, CA
  PROJECT Coach's Calendar 2001
  ART DIRECTOR Suzi McKee
  DESIGNER Vivian Lai
  ILLUSTRATOR Vivian Lai

3 **DESIGN FIRM** The Shamrock Companies Inc., Westlake, OH
  CLIENT Jack Daniels
  PROJECT 2001 Commemorative Calendar
  ART DIRECTOR John Bennett
  DESIGNER John Bennett

4 **DESIGN FIRM** Wee Small Hours Design, New York, NY
  PROJECT Calendar 2000
  ART DIRECTOR Ellen Hibschweiler
  DESIGNERS Saehee Lee, Rie Oshiro

5 **DESIGN FIRM** Zermatt, Luling, LA
  CLIENT Daiquiris
  PROJECT Calendar
  ART DIRECTOR Matt Touchard
  DESIGNER Matt Touchard
  ILLUSTRATOR Matt Touchard

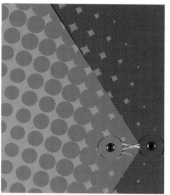

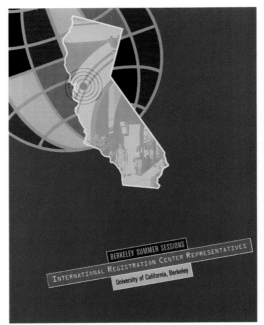

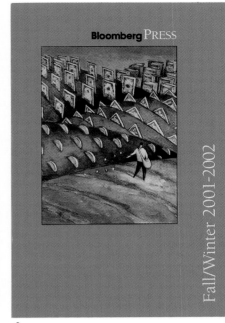

1

2

3

5

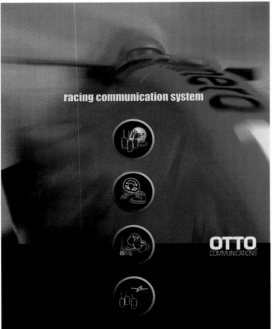

4

1 **DESIGN FIRM** Berkeley Summer Sessions, Berkeley, CA
PROJECT Catalog
ART DIRECTOR Elise Evans
DESIGNER Elise Evans
ILLUSTRATOR David Lance Goines

2 **DESIGN FIRM** Bloomberg, Princeton, NJ
CLIENT Bloomberg Press
PROJECT Catalog Fall/Winter 2001-2002
ART DIRECTOR Sandy O'Connor
DESIGNER Lorraine Kuldanek
ILLUSTRATOR Paul Schulenburg (Cover)

3 **DESIGN FIRM** Casale Design, Inc., New York, NY
CLIENT United States Equestrian Team
PROJECT United States Equestrian Team Catalog - Winter 2001
DESIGNER George T. Casale
PHOTOGRAPHER Dylan Cross, NYC
ILLUSTRATOR Linda Reizen

4 **DESIGN FIRM** E3 Design Group, Elgin, IL
CLIENT Otto Communications
PROJECT Cleartrak Product Catalog
ART DIRECTOR Eric Engelby
DESIGNER Eric Engelby

5 **DESIGN FIRM** Fossil, Inc., Richardson, TX
PROJECT Fossil German Watch Catalog
ART DIRECTOR Stephen Zhang
DESIGNER Dominique Pierron
PHOTOGRAPHER Russ Aman

2

1

1 **DESIGN FIRM** Gammon Ragonesi Associates, New York, NY
CLIENT Skyy Spirits
PROJECT Campari, Aperitif Guide
ART DIRECTOR Mary Ragonesi
DESIGNER Mary Ragonesi
PHOTOGRAPHER Greg Lord

2 **DESIGN FIRM** Getty Images, Seattle, WA
CLIENT Photodisc
PROJECT Juxtapose
ART DIRECTOR Michael Lindsay
DESIGNER Michael Lindsay

3 **DESIGN FIRM** Getty Images, Seattle, WA
CLIENT Artville
PROJECT Catalyst
ART DIRECTOR Michael Lindsay
DESIGNER Heidi Baughman

4 **DESIGN FIRM** Gumption Design, New York, NY
CLIENT Lacoste
PROJECT Look Books 2000
ART DIRECTOR Evelyn Lontok
DESIGNER Evelyn Lontok
PHOTOGRAPHER Marc Anthony

5 **DESIGN FIRM** iDesign, Seymour, CT
CLIENT CrookhomDavis Inc.
PROJECT The Art of Modern Accessories
ART DIRECTOR Nicole Fitzgerald
DESIGNER Nicole Fitzgerald
PHOTOGRAPHER Glen Kapostas-Studio 27

3

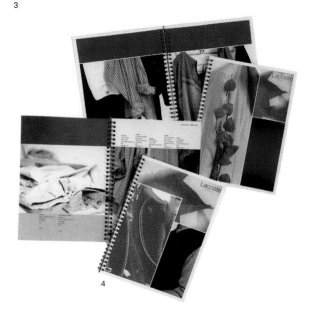

4

5

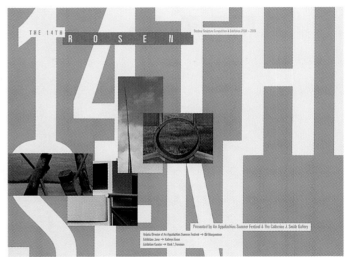

1

2

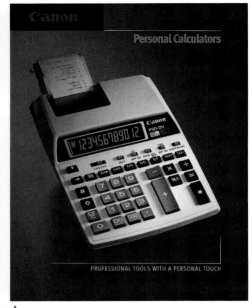

3

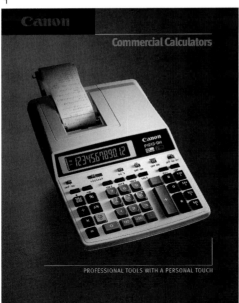

5

4

1 **DESIGN FIRM** Laughing Stock, S. Newfane, VT
PROJECT Catalog No. 8
ART DIRECTOR Carol Ross
DESIGNER Carol Ross
ILLUSTRATOR Jason Schneider (Cover)

2 **DESIGN FIRM** Michael Fanizza Designs, Haslett, MI
CLIENT Catherine J. Smith Gallery, Appalachian State University
PROJECT 14th Rosen Outdoor Sculpture Catalog
ART DIRECTOR Michael Fanizza
DESIGNER Michael Fanizza

3 **DESIGN FIRM** Namaro, Inc., Rhinebeck, NY
CLIENT Canon
PROJECT Commercial Calculators Catalog Series
ART DIRECTOR Nadine Robbins
DESIGNERS Nadine Robbins, Molly Ahearn, Cindy Reifenberger

4 **DESIGN FIRM** Namaro, Inc., Rhinebeck, NY
CLIENT Canon
PROJECT Personal Calculators Catalog Series
ART DIRECTOR Nadine Robbins
DESIGNERS Nadine Robbins, Molly Ahearn, Cindy Reifenberger

5 **DESIGN FIRM** Noevir U.S.A., Inc., Irvine, CA
PROJECT Product Catalog
ART DIRECTOR Joseph Gaydos
DESIGNER Rene Armenta
PHOTOGRAPHERS Greg Porter, Charles Montague
COPYWRITER Hillary Branchflower

1

3

2

4

1 **DESIGN FIRM** Olson, Kotowski & Co., Redondo Beach, CA
CLIENT Boutique Beverly Hills
PROJECT Volume Five, Catalog
ART DIRECTOR Janice Olson
DESIGNER Janice Olson
PHOTOGRAPHER Polara Studios

2 **DESIGN FIRM** Rabid Inc., Warren, OH
CLIENT Mr. Gasket
PROJECT Thundersport Catalog
ART DIRECTOR Kirk Tenney

3 **DESIGN FIRM** Rothstein & Memsic, Los Angeles, CA
CLIENT Asprey & Garrard
PROJECT 2001 Catalog
ART DIRECTOR Jerry Rothstein
DESIGNER Jerry Rothstein
PHOTOGRAPHER Kevin Hecht

4 **DESIGN FIRM** Tribune Media Services, Chicago, IL
CLIENT Zap2it
PROJECT Entertainment Catalog
DESIGNER Stephani Bode Kuehn

"I will not eat oysters. I want my food dead. Not sick, not wounded, dead."

-Woody Allen

1

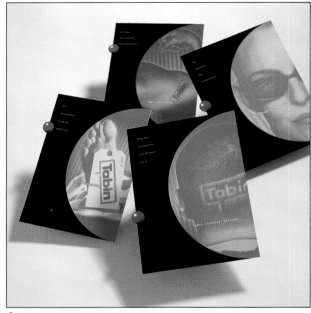

2

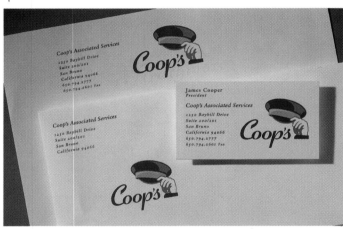

3

4

5

1 **DESIGN FIRM** Belyea, Seattle, WA
   CLIENT VeenendaalCave
   PROJECT Corporate Identity
   ART DIRECTOR Patricia Belyea
   DESIGNER Anne Dougherty

2 **DESIGN FIRM** Brandscope-Chicago, Chicago, IL
   CLIENT Tabin Corporation
   PROJECT Services Promotion
   ART DIRECTOR Bill Harper
   DESIGNERS Susan Hartline-Smith, Annette Ohlsen
   PHOTOGRAPHER Eric Young Smith

3 **DESIGN FIRM** Deutsch Design Works, San Francisco, CA
   CLIENT Coop's Services
   PROJECT Coop's Skycap Services
   ART DIRECTOR Barry Deutsch
   DESIGNER Jess Giambroni
   ILLUSTRATOR Jess Giambroni

4 **DESIGN FIRM** DNO Productions Inc., San Francisco, CA
   PROJECT Corporate Identity
   ART DIRECTOR Keith Hart

5 **DESIGN FIRM** EPOS, Inc., Santa Monica, CA
   CLIENT Roland Corporation USA
   PROJECT Roland Book 2000
   ART DIRECTOR Gabrielle Raumberger
   DESIGNER Eric Martinez

1

2

3

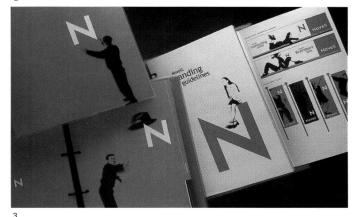

4

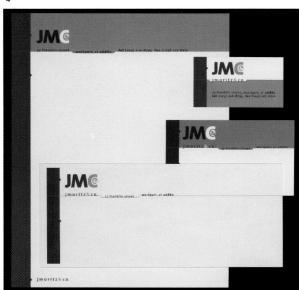

5

1 **DESIGN FIRM** frog design, Sunnyvale, CA
CLIENT Intershop
PROJECT Corporate Identity and Collateral
ART DIRECTOR Gregory Hom
DESIGNERS Hafez Janssens, Roger Siu, Paul Obleas, Matt Roblee

2 **DESIGN FIRM** Hornall Anderson Design Works, Inc., Seattle, WA
CLIENT Space Needle
PROJECT Identity Program
ART DIRECTOR Jack Anderson
DESIGNERS Jack Anderson, Mary Hermes, Gretchen Cook, Andrew Smith, Julie Lock, Holly Craven, Elmer Dela Cruz, Belinda Bowling, Amy Faucette, Alan Florsheim, Cliff Chung
NAMING/BRANDING CONSULTANT Tyler Cartier

3 **DESIGN FIRM** Hornall Anderson Design Works, Inc., Seattle, WA
CLIENT Novell, Inc.
PROJECT 2001 Corporate Identity Program
ART DIRECTORS Jack Anderson, Larry Anderson
DESIGNERS Larry Anderson, James Tee, Holly Craven, Michael Brugman, Kaye Farmer, Cliff Chung, Taka Suzuki, Belinda Bowling, Jay Hilburn
PHOTOGRAPHER David Emitte

4 **DESIGN FIRM** Lipset Design Studio, Wilton, CT
PROJECT Corporate Identity
ART DIRECTOR Jennifer Lipset
DESIGNER Jennifer Lipset

5 **DESIGN FIRM** Lipset Design Studio, Wilton, CT
CLIENT Jmoritz & Co.
PROJECT Corporate Identity
ART DIRECTOR Jennifer Lipset
DESIGNER Jennifer Lipset

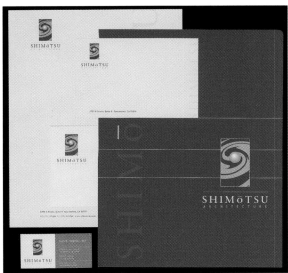

2

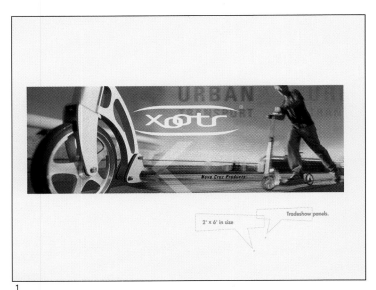

1

3

5

1 **DESIGN FIRM** Lunar Design, San Francisco, CA
   CLIENT Nova Cruz Products
   PROJECT Xootr Brand Development
   ART DIRECTOR Kristen Bailey
   DESIGNERS Flo Bautista, Becky Brown

2 **DESIGN FIRM** Page Design, Inc., Sacramento, CA
   CLIENT Shimotsu Architecture
   PROJECT Business System & Collateral
   ART DIRECTORS Paul Page, Chris Brown
   DESIGNER Chris Brown
   ILLUSTRATOR Chris Brown

3 **DESIGN FIRM** Rule 29, Elgin, IL
   PROJECT Corporate Identity
   ART DIRECTORS Justin Ahrens, Jim Boborci
   DESIGNERS Justin Ahrens, Jim Boborci

4 **DESIGN FIRM** Sherman Advertising, New York, NY
   CLIENT Roseland Property
   PROJECT Jumping Brook Stationery
   ART DIRECTOR Sharon Elaine Lloyd
   DESIGNER Sharon Elaine Lloyd
   ILLUSTRATOR Westley Bates

5 **DESIGN FIRM** Smith Design Associates, Bloomfield, NJ
   CLIENT Scholastic
   PROJECT Scholastic Brand Manual
   ART DIRECTOR James C. Smith
   DESIGNER Eileen Berezni
   ILLUSTRATOR Eileen Berezni

1

2

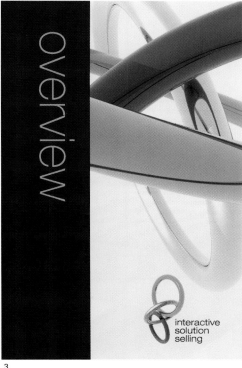

3

4

1 **DESIGN FIRM** Tamada Brown & Associates, Chicago, IL
  CLIENT Infocrossing
  PROJECT Identity
  ART DIRECTOR Phyliss Tamada-Brown
  DESIGNER Andy Wong

2 **DESIGN FIRM** The Weber Group, Inc., Racine, WI
  CLIENT Johnson Wax Professional
  PROJECT Corporate Identity
  ART DIRECTOR Anthony Weber
  DESIGNER Anthony Weber

3 **DESIGN FIRM** Towers Perrin, Chicago, IL
  CLIENT Astra Zeneca
  PROJECT Interactive Solution Selling Tool Kit
  ART DIRECTOR Mary Endress
  DESIGNERS Jonathan Harris, Rick Mank

4 **DESIGN FIRM** Zamboo, Marina Del Rey, CA
  CLIENT PMLA
  PROJECT Corporate Identity
  DESIGNER Dave Zambotti

AT LEAST IF THE CLIENT REJECTS IT,

YOU'LL HAVE A GREAT PIECE

FOR YOUR BOOK.

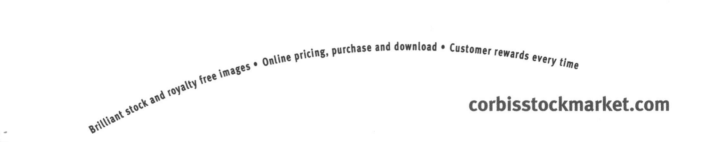

© Mark Tuschman 0-029-0601 ©2001 Corbis Corporation

Corbis Stock Market. Visually driven. **800.999.0800**

Brilliant stock and royalty free images • Online pricing, purchase and download • Customer rewards every time

corbisstockmarket.com

Corbis·
STOCK MARKET

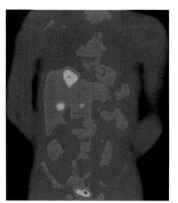

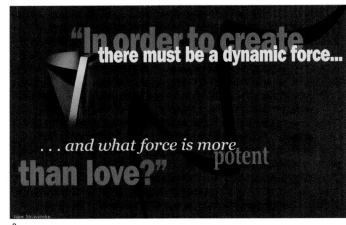

2

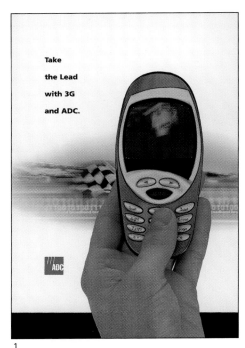

1

3

4

1 **DESIGN FIRM** ADC Creative Services Group, Eden Prairie, MN
PROJECT 3G Direct Mail Ad
ART DIRECTOR Curt Erickson
DESIGNER ADC Creative Group
PHOTOGRAPHER Mike McCann

2 **DESIGN FIRM** Amazing Spaces, Bear Creek, PA
CLIENT Marketechs, Inc.
PROJECT Intro Teaser Mail Campaign
ART DIRECTOR Michelle Evans
DESIGNER Michelle Evans
PHOTOGRAPHER Alan Wycheck

3 **DESIGN FIRM** Brierley & Partners, Los Angeles, CA
CLIENT Epson
PROJECT Epson Stylus Pro 5500
ART DIRECTORS Rusty Sanchez, Donna Johnston

4 **DESIGN FIRM** Brierley & Partners, Los Angeles, CA
CLIENT Epson
PROJECT Epson Expression 1640XL
ART DIRECTORS Rusty Sanchez, Donna Johnston

5 **DESIGN FIRM** Citigate Albert Frank, New York, NY
PROJECT Venture Capitalist Mailing
ART DIRECTOR Vlad Kogan
CREATIVE DIRECTOR Joshua Altman
COPYWRITER Kira O'Sullivan

5

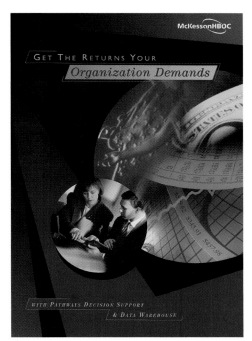

1

2

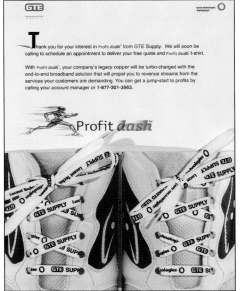

3

1 **DESIGN FIRM** Crawford/Mikus Design, Inc., Atlanta, GA
CLIENT APG-ITB
PROJECT Direct Mail
ART DIRECTOR Elizabeth Crawford
DESIGNER Elizabeth Crawford
ILLUSTRATOR Elizabeth Crawford

2 **DESIGN FIRM** DCI Marketing, Milwaukee, WI
CLIENT Harley-Davidson Motorcycles
PROJECT Service Reminder Spring 2001
ART DIRECTOR Alan Eliason
DESIGNER Alan Eliason
COPY Alan Eliason

3 **DESIGN FIRM** Hull Creative Group, Boston, MA
CLIENT Pearson Publishing
PROJECT CD Mailer
CREATIVE DIRECTOR Carolyn Hull
DESIGNER Amy Braddock

4 **DESIGN FIRM** JA Design Solutions, Coppell, TX
CLIENT GTE Supply
PROJECT GTE Supply-Lucent DSL
ART DIRECTOR Jean Ashenfelter
DESIGNER Jean Ashenfelter

5 **DESIGN FIRM** Maru Leon Design, New York, NY
CLIENT George Magazine
PROJECT Direct Mail Promotion
ART DIRECTOR Maru Leon
DESIGNER Emily De Sear

4

5

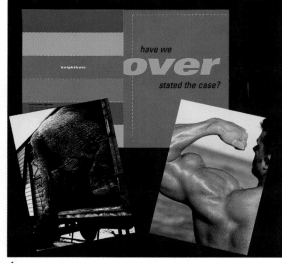

1

2

3

4

5

1 **DESIGN FIRM** Nesnadny + Schwartz
CLIENT SMART Papers
ART DIRECTORS Joyce Nesnadny, Michelle Moehler
DESIGNER Michelle Moehler
PHOTOGRAPHERS Alex Ardenti Photography, Ron Stewart, Raoul Gradvohl, Henry Horenstein, Design Photography Inc.

2 **DESIGN FIRM** Skidmore Inc., Southfield, MI
CLIENT MVP Communications
PROJECT MVP and the Fine Art of Moving
ART DIRECTOR Mae Skidmore
DESIGNER John Latin
PHOTOGRAPHER Jeff Hargis

3 **DESIGN FIRM** Tabara Design, San Jose, CA
PROJECT Postcards
ART DIRECTOR Kyoto Tabara Dougherty
DESIGNER Kyoto Tabara Dougherty

4 **DESIGN FIRM** The Indigo Group, Shelton, CT
CLIENT Brand Direct Marketing
PROJECT Disney Adventure Club
ART DIRECTOR Dawn Tufano
DESIGNER Dawn Tufano
ILLUSTRATOR Dawn Tufano

5 **DESIGN FIRM** Tony Mistretta Graphics, Chicago, IL
CLIENT Bill Jacobs VW-Aurora
PROJECT Direct Mail Program
DESIGNER Patrick Kelly

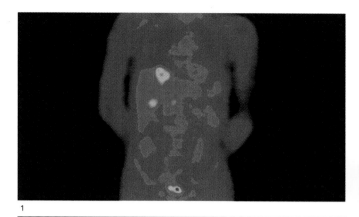

1

2

3

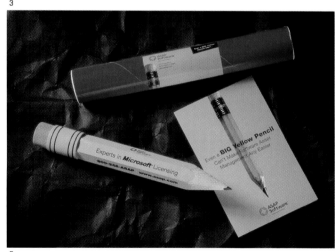

4

5

1 **DESIGN FIRM** trgMarketing Works, York, PA
CLIENT Tristan Associates
PROJECT PET Imaging Mailer
ART DIRECTOR Martin Bentley Krebs
DESIGNER Martin Bentley Krebs

2 **DESIGN FIRM** Tribune Media Services, Chicago, IL
CLIENT KRTi Hot Topics
PROJECT Where Do You Turn if You Don't Want to Burn?
DESIGNER Ji Kim

3 **DESIGN FIRM** Tribune Media Services, Chicago, IL
CLIENT Film File Direct
PROJECT Oscar Pre-Show Card
ART DIRECTOR Lyle Anderson
DESIGNER Lyly Anderson

4 **DESIGN FIRM** Unigraphics, Inc., Dallas, TX
CLIENT Dallas Summer Musicals
PROJECT Here's the Scoop for Our 61st Summer Season
ART DIRECTOR Bonnie Evans
DESIGNER Bonnie Evans
PHOTOGRAPHER Tom Welch
ILLUSTRATOR Clay McClure

5 **DESIGN FIRM** ZGraphics, Ltd., East Dundee, IL
CLIENT ASAP Software
PROJECT Government CIO Pencil Mailer
ART DIRECTOR Joe Zeller
DESIGNER Nate Baron
ILLUSTRATOR Tumbaugh Illustration

WE'RE OBSESSED WITH OUR IMAGE

Photo: Ann Summa

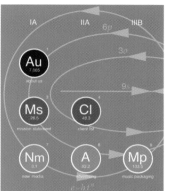

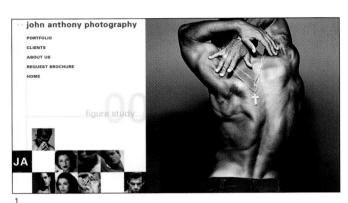

1

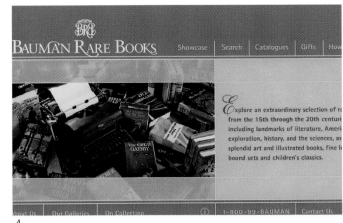

2

3

4

5

1 **DESIGN FIRM** 2Sisters Design, Redwood Shores, CA
CLIENT John Anthony Photography
PROJECT Web Site
ART DIRECTORS Karen Uhl Van, Jennifer Uhl Maurray
DESIGNERS Karen Uhl Van, Jennifer Uhl Maurray
PHOTOGRAPHER John Anthony

2 **DESIGN FIRM** ad2, Inc., Santa Monica, CA
CLIENT Columbia TriStar Film Distributors International
PROJECT www.crouchingtiger.com
ART DIRECTOR Justin Kuzmanich
DESIGNER Justin Kuzmanich
PROGRAMMER Matt Minich

3 **DESIGN FIRM** atCommunications, LLC, Oakbrook Terrace, IL
CLIENT Clayton Metals, Inc.
PROJECT Animated Splash Page
DESIGNER Terry P. Kasdan

4 **DESIGN FIRM** Axium Studio Inc., Philadelphia, PA
CLIENT Bauman Rare Books
PROJECT Web Site
ART DIRECTOR Michael McDonald
DESIGNER A.J. Melvin

5 **DESIGN FIRM** BTD, New York, NY
CLIENT Andrea Sperling
PROJECT Web Site
ART DIRECTOR Beth Tondreau
DESIGNER Lorie Pagnozzi
PHOTOGRAPHER Andrea Sperling

1

2

3

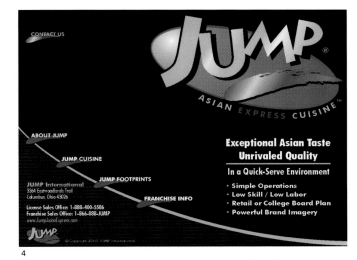

4

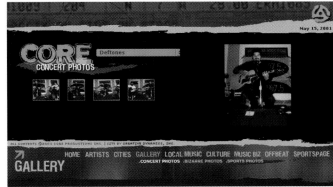

5

1 **DESIGN FIRM** Capisce Design, Los Angeles, CA
PROJECT Web Site
ART DIRECTOR Tracy Man

2 **DESIGN FIRM** Capital Associated Industries, Raleigh, NC
CLIENT Planworx Architecture
PROJECT Web Site
ART DIRECTOR Stephen McCulloch
DESIGNER Stephen McCulloch

3 **DESIGN FIRM** Casale Design, Inc., New York, NY
CLIENT Gargiulo's Restaurant
PROJECT Gargiulo's Restaurant Web Site
DESIGNER George T. Casale
COPY Nino Russo

4 **DESIGN FIRM** Creative Design Solutions, Columbus, OH
CLIENT Jump International
PROJECT Web Site
ART DIRECTOR Chris Schweitzer
DESIGNERS Chris Schweitzer, Jon Herman
PHOTOGRAPHER Laura Sifferlin

5 **DESIGN FIRM** Creative Dynamics, Inc., Las Vegas, NV
CLIENT Core Productions
PROJECT coredistortion.com
ART DIRECTORS Eddie Roberts, Victor Rodriguez
DESIGNER Casey Corcoran

4

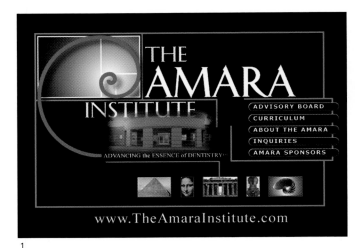

1

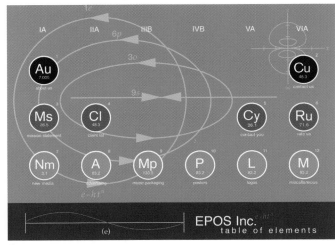

5

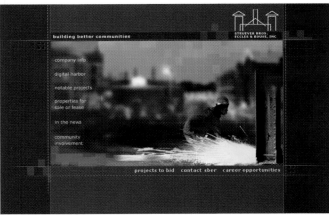

2

3

1 **DESIGN FIRM** Curtis Marketing Group, St. Joseph, MN
   CLIENT The Amara Institute
   PROJECT Home Page
   ART DIRECTOR Michael White
   DESIGNER Michael White

2 **DESIGN FIRM** Design Guys, Minneapolis, MN
   CLIENT Hest & Kramer
   PROJECT Web Site
   ART DIRECTOR Steven Sikora
   DESIGNERS Jay Theige, Ollie Bauer

3 **DESIGN FIRM** e.magination, Baltimore, MD
   CLIENT Struever Bros. Eccles & Rouse, Inc.
   PROJECT Web Site
   DESIGNER Beth Mullin

4 **DESIGN FIRM** EPOS, Inc., Santa Monica, CA
   PROJECT Corporate Web Site
   ART DIRECTOR Gabrielle Raumberger
   DESIGNER Clifford Singontiko

5 **DESIGN FIRM** Goldfish Productions, Rutland, VT
   PROJECT Web Site
   ART DIRECTOR Pam Rice
   DESIGNER Pam Rice
   PHOTOGRAPHER Steve Kent

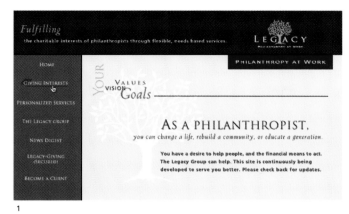

1

2

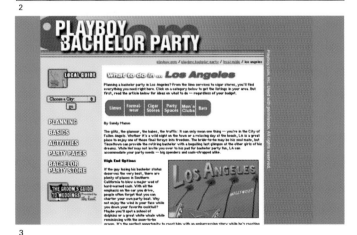

3

4

5

1 **DESIGN FIRM** Hare Strigenz Design, Inc., Milwaukee, WI
CLIENT The Legacy Group
PROJECT Web Site
ART DIRECTOR Paula Hare
DESIGNER Nicole Vogt

2 **DESIGN FIRM** ignition13 inc., Stamford, CT
CLIENT Giovanni Pagnotta
PROJECT Web Site
DESIGNER ignition13 inc.

3 **DESIGN FIRM** Ken Smith Illustration, Chicago, IL
CLIENT Playboy.com
PROJECT Bachelor Party Postcards
ART DIRECTOR Jay Boersing
DESIGNER Don Schnitzius
ILLUSTRATOR Ken Smith

4 **DESIGN FIRM** Lunar Design, San Francisco, CA
PROJECT Web Site
DESIGNER Lunar Design Team

5 **DESIGN FIRM** Marriott International, Washington, DC
CLIENT Marriott Northeast Region
PROJECT New England Microsite
ART DIRECTOR Jeff Dickshinski
DESIGNER Beth Santos

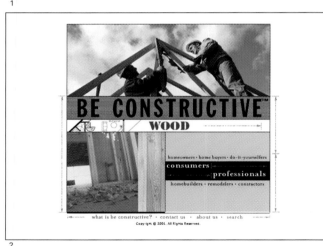

1 **DESIGN FIRM** Marriott International, Washington, DC
PROJECT Meeting Planner Microsite
ART DIRECTOR Jeff Dickshinski
DESIGNER Elaine Faye

2 **DESIGN FIRM** Mullen, Pittsburgh, PA
CLIENT be constructive
PROJECT Web Site
ART DIRECTORS Jay Carol, Nathan Kress
DESIGNERS Nick Cobler, Nathan Kress

3 **DESIGN FIRM** Mullen, Pittsburgh, PA
CLIENT Wine Market Council
PROJECT Web Site
ART DIRECTORS Jay Good, Nathan Kress
DESIGNERS Nick Cobler, Ted Williams

4 **DESIGN FIRM** New York City Economic Development Corporation
PROJECT Web Site
ART DIRECTOR Cindy Parsons
DESIGNER Cindy Parsons

5 **DESIGN FIRM** Orbit Integrated, Hockessin, DE
CLIENT WebMiles
PROJECT Web Site
ART DIRECTORS Jack Harris, Bill Harris
DESIGNERS Charlie Bacon, Ed Abbott
PHOTOGRAPHER Carlos Alejandro

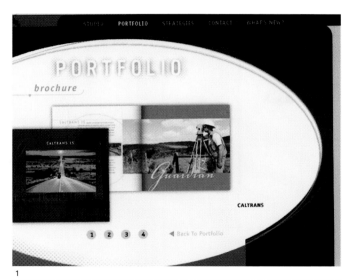

1

2

3

4

5

1 **DESIGN FIRM** Page Design, Inc., Sacramento, CA
PROJECT Web Site
ART DIRECTOR Paul Page
DESIGNER Kurt Kland
PHOTOGRAPHER Gordon Lazzarone Photography
ILLUSTRATOR Kurt Kland

2 **DESIGN FIRM** Red Stone New Media, Houston, TX
CLIENT Ferrell North America
PROJECT Web Site
ART DIRECTOR Tommy Leo
DESIGNER Tommy Leo

3 **DESIGN FIRM** Robert Llewellyn Photographer, Earlysville, VA
PROJECT Web Site
ART DIRECTOR Robert Llewellyn
DESIGNER Robert Llewellyn
PHOTOGRAPHER Robert Llewellyn

4 **DESIGN FIRM** SCK Design Inc., Cleveland, OH
CLIENT Lake Ridge Academy
PROJECT Web Site
DESIGNER Xenia Rivera

5 **DESIGN FIRM** SWT Media Services, San Marcos, TX
CLIENT SWT Geography Department
PROJECT Department of Geography Web Site
ART DIRECTOR Teri Andrews
DESIGNER Teri Andrews
PHOTOGRAPHER Robert Alexander Williams
PRODUCTION ARTISTS Nancy Bigelow, Samuel Trim, Earl Hopkins

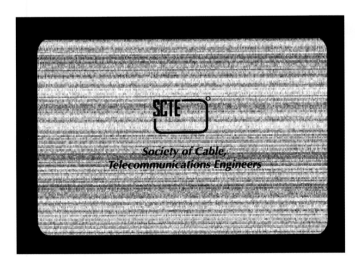

1

2

4

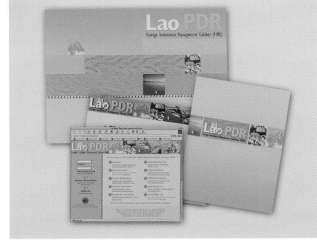

5

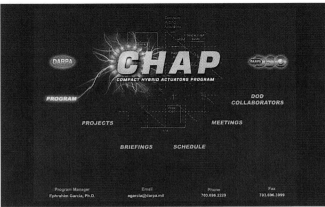

3

1   **DESIGN FIRM** TGD Communications, Inc., Alexandria, VA
    CLIENT Society of Cable, Telecommunications Engineers
    PROJECT SCTE Flash Intro
    ART DIRECTOR Chris Harrison
    DESIGNER Chris Harrison

2   **DESIGN FIRM** The Media Game®, Miami Beach, FL
    PROJECT Web Site
    ART DIRECTOR Christina Ricci
    DESIGNER Christina Ricci

3   **DESIGN FIRM** Walcoff Technologies, Fairfax, VA
    CLIENT DARPA Defense Sciences Office
    PROJECT Compact Hybrid Actuators Program Web Site
    ART DIRECTOR David Hoff
    DESIGNERS Joshua Kinberg, Vithaya Phongsavan

4   **DESIGN FIRM** Walcoff Technologies, Fairfax, VA
    CLIENT DARPA Defense Sciences Office
    PROJECT Palm Power Program Web Site
    ART DIRECTOR David Hoff
    DESIGNERS Vithaya Phongsavan, David Hoff

5   **DESIGN FIRM** Wee Small Hours Design, New York, NY
    CLIENT MIGA, The World Bank Group
    PROJECT Indochina Web Development - Lao PDR
    ART DIRECTOR Ellen Hibschweiler
    DESIGNER Saehee Lee

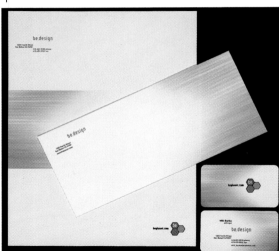

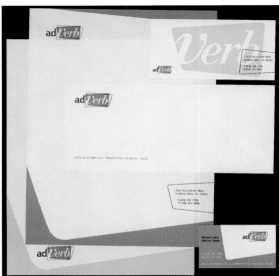

1 **DESIGN FIRM** 818 Studio Inc., Annapolis, MD
   CLIENT Horizon Builders
   PROJECT Stationery
   DESIGNER Keith Johnston

2 **DESIGN FIRM** ad2, Inc., Santa Monica, CA
   PROJECT New Stationery Design
   ART DIRECTOR Justin Kuzmanich
   DESIGNERS Justin Kuzmanich, David Brady

3 **DESIGN FIRM** Barnett Design, Inc., Ramsey, NJ
   CLIENT Buckwalter Law, PC
   PROJECT Stationery Kit, Logo
   ART DIRECTOR Debra Barnett Sagurton
   DESIGNER Jefferson Ramos

4 **DESIGN FIRM** be•design, San Rafael, CA
   PROJECT Letterhead and Stationery
   ART DIRECTORS Will Burke, Eric Read
   DESIGNERS Coralie Russo, Yusuke Asaka

5 **DESIGN FIRM** be•design, San Rafael, CA
   CLIENT ad Verb
   PROJECT Letterhead and Stationery
   ART DIRECTOR Eric Read
   DESIGNERS Eric Read, Yusuke Asaka

2

1

3

1 **DESIGN FIRM** be•design, San Rafael, CA
   CLIENT Audiobase
   PROJECT Letterhead and Stationery
   ART DIRECTOR Will Burke
   DESIGNERS Eric Read, Yusuke Asaka, Jeff Martel

2 **DESIGN FIRM** Capisce Design, Los Angeles, CA
   CLIENT I of a Kind Jewelry Designs, Inc.
   PROJECT Alien 2000 Business Card
   ART DIRECTOR Tracy Man

3 **DESIGN FIRM** Capital Associated Industries, Raleigh, NC
   CLIENT Netherwood Productions
   PROJECT Stationery
   ART DIRECTOR Beth Greene
   DESIGNER Beth Greene
   ILLUSTRATOR Beth Greene

4 **DESIGN FIRM** Chebacco Design & Communications, LLC, Hamilton, MA
   CLIENT The Remodeling Company
   PROJECT Stationery
   ART DIRECTOR Chuck Carey
   DESIGNERS Chuck Carey, Evan Sanderson
   ILLUSTRATOR Evan Sanderson

5 **DESIGN FIRM** Cisneros Design, Inc., Santa Fe, NM
   PROJECT Stationery Package
   ART DIRECTOR Brian Hurshman
   DESIGNER Brian Hurshman

4

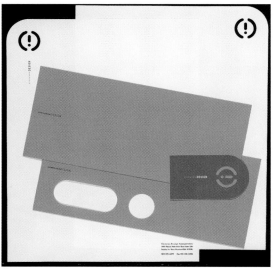

5

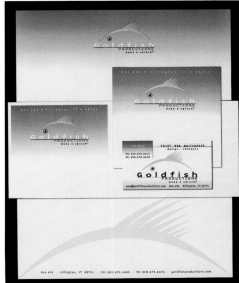

1 **DESIGN FIRM** D4 Creative Group, Philadelphia, PA
  PROJECT Stationery
  ART DIRECTOR Wicky Lee

2 **DESIGN FIRM** Design Matters Inc!, New York, NY
  CLIENT Nuveen Investments
  PROJECT Stationery
  ART DIRECTOR Stephen McAllister
  DESIGNER Stephen McAllister

3 **DESIGN FIRM** Goldfish Productions, Rutland, VT
  PROJECT Corporate Stationery
  ART DIRECTOR Pam Rice
  DESIGNER Pam Rice
  ILLUSTRATOR Pam Rice

4 **DESIGN FIRM** Gomersall Design, Santa Barbara, CA
  CLIENT Arcadia Studio
  PROJECT Stationery
  ART DIRECTOR Dianne Gomersall
  DESIGNER Dianne Gomersall
  ILLUSTRATOR Dianne Gomersall

5 **DESIGN FIRM** Greenfield/Belser Ltd., Washington, DC
  CLIENT Blue Chair Design
  PROJECT Stationery
  ART DIRECTOR Burkey Belser
  DESIGNER Stephanie Fernandez
  ILLUSTRATOR Tom Cauler

2

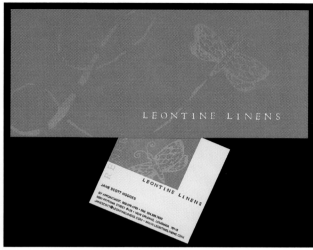

1

3

1 **DESIGN FIRM** H, New Orleans, LA
CLIENT Leontine Linens
PROJECT Stationery
ART DIRECTOR Winnie Hart
DESIGNERS Winnie Hart, Gaby Tillero

2 **DESIGN FIRM** HC Creative Communications, Bethesda, MD
CLIENT CoreFacts
PROJECT Stationery
ART DIRECTOR Howard Clare
DESIGNER Jessica Palombo

3 **DESIGN FIRM** Hornall Anderson Design Works, Inc., Seattle, WA
CLIENT Aerzone
PROJECT Stationery Program
ART DIRECTOR Mark Popich
DESIGNERS Mark Popich, Mary McCafferty, Ed Lee, Gretchen Cook, Andrew Smith

4 **DESIGN FIRM** Hornall Anderson Design Works, Inc., Seattle, WA
CLIENT XOW!
PROJECT Stationery Program
ART DIRECTORS Jack Anderson, Lisa Cerveny
DESIGNERS Lisa Cerveny, Bruce Branson-Meyer, Jana Nishi, Mary Chin Hutchison, Don Stayner

5 **DESIGN FIRM** Hornall Anderson Design Works, Inc., Seattle, WA
CLIENT Freerein
PROJECT Stationery Program
ART DIRECTOR Jack Anderson
DESIGNERS John Anderle, Gretchen Cook, Mark Popich, Tobi Brown,
John Anicker, Steffanie Lorig, Bruce Stigler, Ensi Mofasser, Elmer Dela Cruz

4

5

1

2

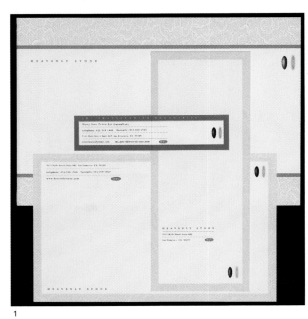

3

1 **DESIGN FIRM** Hornall Anderson Design Works, Inc., Seattle, WA
   CLIENT Heavenly Stone
   PROJECT Stationery Program
   ART DIRECTOR Jack Anderson
   DESIGNERS Jack Anderson, Henry Yiu
   CALLIGRAPHY Taka Suzuki

2 **DESIGN FIRM** Hornall Anderson Design Works, Inc., Seattle, WA
   CLIENT Widmer Brothers
   PROJECT Stationery Program
   ART DIRECTORS Jack Anderson, Larry Anderson
   DESIGNERS Jack Anderson, Larry Anderson, Ed Lee, Bruce Stigler, Bruce
   Branson-Meyer, Mary Chin Hutchison, Michael Brugman, Kaye Farmer

3 **DESIGN FIRM** Hornall Anderson Design Works, Inc., Seattle, WA
   CLIENT Twelve Horses
   PROJECT Stationery Program
   ART DIRECTOR Jack Anderson
   DESIGNERS Jack Anderson, Mary Chin Hutchison, Lisa Cerveny, Don Stayner

4 **DESIGN FIRM** ignition13 inc., Stamford, CT
   PROJECT Identity System
   DESIGNER ignition13 inc.

5 **DESIGN FIRM** Kircher, Washington, DC
   CLIENT HireRight, LLC
   PROJECT Stationery
   ART DIRECTOR Bruce E. Morgan
   DESIGNER Bruce E. Morgan

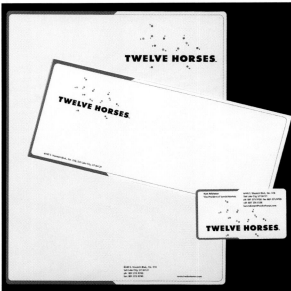

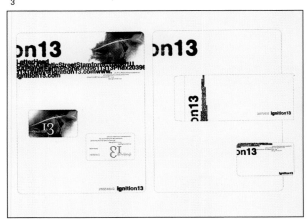

4

5

1

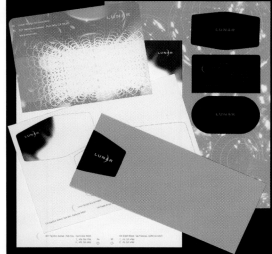

2

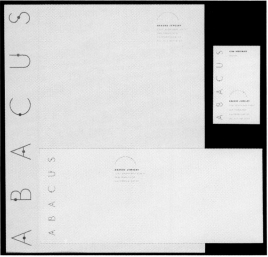

3

4

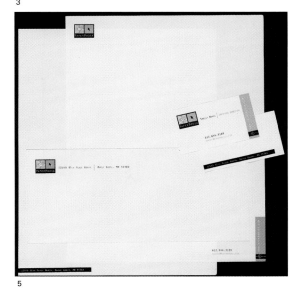

5

1 **DESIGN FIRM** Lesniewicz Associates, Toledo, OH
   CLIENT Golden Retriever Rescue of Michigan
   PROJECT Stationery
   ART DIRECTOR Terry Lesniewicz
   DESIGNER Amy Lesniewicz

2 **DESIGN FIRM** Lunar Design, San Francisco, CA
   PROJECT Business System
   DESIGNERS Flo Bautista, Becky Brown, Ed Serapio

3 **DESIGN FIRM** Mark Selfe Design, Emeryville, CA
   CLIENT newmoon.com
   PROJECT Stationery System
   ART DIRECTOR Mark Selfe
   DESIGNER Mark Selfe

4 **DESIGN FIRM** Mark Selfe Design, Emeryville, CA
   CLIENT Abacus Jewelry
   PROJECT Stationery System
   ART DIRECTOR Mark Selfe
   DESIGNER Mark Selfe

5 **DESIGN FIRM** PaperMouse, Maple Grove, MN
   PROJECT Stationery
   ART DIRECTOR Shelly Hokel
   DESIGNER Shelly Hokel
   ILLUSTRATOR Shelly Hokel

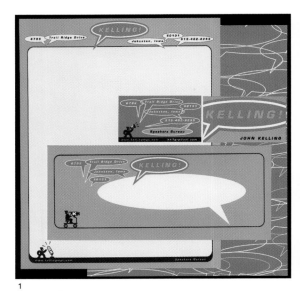

2

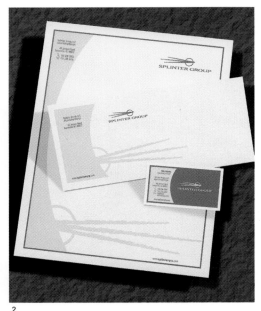

1

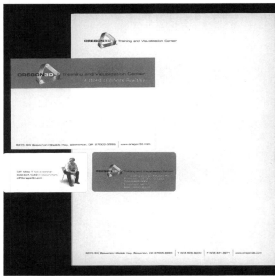

3

4

1 **DESIGN FIRM** Sayles Graphic Design, Des Moines, IA
  CLIENT Kelling Management Group
  PROJECT Letterhead
  ART DIRECTOR John Sayles
  DESIGNER John Sayles
  ILLUSTRATOR John Sayles

2 **DESIGN FIRM** Splinter Group, Sayreville, NJ
  PROJECT Letterhead
  ART DIRECTOR Rob Adams

3 **DESIGN FIRM** Staccato Design, Portland, OR
  CLIENT Oregon 3D
  PROJECT Identity
  ART DIRECTOR Christopher Douglas
  DESIGNER Christopher Douglas

4 **DESIGN FIRM** Studio North, North Chicago, IL
  CLIENT Visual Insights
  PROJECT Stationery
  ART DIRECTOR Mark Schneider
  DESIGNER Erik Peterson

5 **DESIGN FIRM** Suktion Production, Laguna Beach, CA
  PROJECT Letterhead
  ART DIRECTOR Alex Melli
  DESIGNER Doug Bradshaw
  PHOTOGRAPHER Alex Melli
  ILLUSTRATOR Alex Melli

5

1

2

3

4

1 **DESIGN FIRM** Tamada Brown & Associates, Chicago, IL
CLIENT ForeFront Education
PROJECT Stationery
ART DIRECTOR Robert Brown
DESIGNER Andy Wong

2 **DESIGN FIRM** VLM Studios, Miami, FL
CLIENT ADX Technologies
PROJECT Stationery
ART DIRECTOR Vanessa Lam-Mendieta
DESIGNER Vanessa Lam-Mendieta
ILLUSTRATOR Vanessa Lam-Mendieta

3 **DESIGN FIRM** Wallace Church, Inc., New York, NY
PROJECT Stationery System
ART DIRECTORS Stan Church, Nin Glaister
DESIGNERS Nin Glaister, Lawrence Haggerty
PHOTOGRAPHER Marcus Bertschi
PRODUCTION Susan Wiley

4 **DESIGN FIRM** Zeesman Communications, Culver City, CA
PROJECT Letterhead & Stationery
ART DIRECTOR Trish Abbot
DESIGNER Trish Abbot

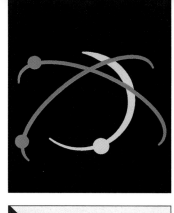

1

2

3

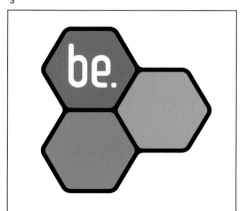

4

5

6

7

8

1 **DESIGN FIRM** Amazing Spaces, Bear Creek, PA
CLIENT Marketechs, Inc.
PROJECT Logo
ART DIRECTOR Michelle Evans
DESIGNER Michelle Evans

2 **DESIGN FIRM** Bailey Design Group,
Plymouth Meeting, PA
CLIENT CPG Technologies
PROJECT FreshSeal Identity
ART DIRECTOR Dave Fiedler
DESIGNERS Ken Cahill, Ann Marie Malone

3 **DESIGN FIRM** BD&E, Pittsburgh, PA
CLIENT Watson Institute
PROJECT Logo
ART DIRECTOR Jeff Piatt
DESIGNER Anne Flanagan
ILLUSTRATOR Anne Flanagan

4 **DESIGN FIRM** be•design, San Rafael, CA
PROJECT Logo
ART DIRECTOR Will Burke
DESIGNERS Eric Read, Yusuke Asaka

5 **DESIGN FIRM** be•design, San Rafael, CA
CLIENT Microsoft (Ultimate TV)
PROJECT Logo
ART DIRECTOR Will Burke
DESIGNERS Eric Read, Yusuke Asaka

6 **DESIGN FIRM** be•design, San Rafael, CA
CLIENT Worldwise, Inc.
PROJECT Logo
ART DIRECTOR Will Burke
DESIGNERS Eric Read, Yusuke Asaka,
Coralie Russo

7 **DESIGN FIRM** be•design, San Rafael, CA
CLIENT Mr. Swap (e-commerce)
PROJECT Logo
ART DIRECTOR Will Burke
DESIGNERS Eric Read, Yusuke Asaka, John Meeks
ILLUSTRATOR Yusuke Asaka

8 **DESIGN FIRM** BOLT, Charlotte, NC
CLIENT Lance
PROJECT Thunder Product Identity
ART DIRECTOR John Baker
DESIGNER Sarah Konieczny

1

2

3

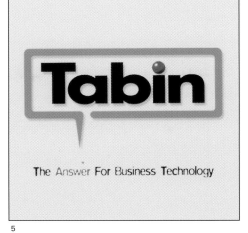

4

5

6

7

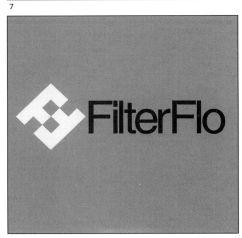

8

1 **DESIGN FIRM** Boyd Communications,
Los Angeles, CA
CLIENT Pure Fishing
PROJECT Logo
ART DIRECTOR Randall Momii
DESIGNER Randall Momii
ILLUSTRATOR Randall Momii

2 **DESIGN FIRM** Boyd Communications,
Los Angeles, CA
CLIENT Hilton Hotels
PROJECT CCC&S Logo
ART DIRECTOR Randall Momii
DESIGNER Randall Momii
ILLUSTRATOR Randall Momii

3 **DESIGN FIRM** Brandscope-Chicago, Chicago, IL
CLIENT Radio-Flyer
PROJECT Icon
ART DIRECTOR Bill Harper
DESIGNER Bill Harper

4 **DESIGN FIRM** Brandscope-Chicago, Chicago, IL
CLIENT I-GO
PROJECT Corporate Identity
ART DIRECTOR Bill Harper
DESIGNER Susan Hartline-Smith

5 **DESIGN FIRM** Brandscope-Chicago, Chicago, IL
CLIENT Tabin Corporation
PROJECT Brand Identity
ART DIRECTOR Bill Harper
DESIGNER Bill Harper

6 **DESIGN FIRM** Brian J. Ganton & Associates,
Cedar Grove, NJ
CLIENT United States Tobacco International, Inc.
PROJECT Habano Primero Logo
ART DIRECTOR Christopher Ganton
DESIGNER Christopher Ganton
CREATIVE DIRECTOR Brian Ganton, Jr.
ILLUSTRATOR Juan Lee

7 **DESIGN FIRM** Chebacco Design &
Communications, LLC, Hamilton, MA
CLIENT The Remodeling Company
PROJECT Logo
ART DIRECTOR Chuck Carey
DESIGNERS Chuck Carey, Evan Sanderson
ILLUSTRATOR Evan Sanderson

8 **DESIGN FIRM** Chebacco Design &
Communications, LLC, Hamilton, MA
CLIENT Filter Flo
PROJECT Logo
ART DIRECTOR Chuck Carey
DESIGNER Chuck Carey
ILLUSTRATOR Chuck Carey

Pre-D Systems™
The Winds of Change
Begin With a Flutter…

4

1

2

3

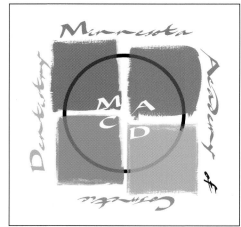

5

6

7

8

1 **DESIGN FIRM** Cornerstone Design Associates,
New York, NY
CLIENT Telemig
PROJECT W. Aura Brand Identity Development
ART DIRECTORS Keith Steimel, Sally Clarke
DESIGNERS Sarah Janson, Frank Yang, Mo Pizzi,
Nicole Libshik

2 **DESIGN FIRM** Crawford/Mikus Design, Inc.,
Atlanta, GA
CLIENT Houston Mill House
PROJECT Identity
ART DIRECTOR Elizabeth Crawford
DESIGNER Elizabeth Crawford
ILLUSTRATOR Elizabeth Crawford

3 **DESIGN FIRM** Creative Dynamics, Inc.,
Las Vegas, NV
CLIENT Tumak's Bar and Grill
PROJECT Logo
ART DIRECTORS Victor Rodriguez, Eddie Roberts
DESIGNER Eddie Roberts
ILLUSTRATOR Eddie Roberts

4 **DESIGN FIRM** Curtis Marketing Group,
St. Joseph, MN
CLIENT Pre-D Systems
PROJECT Logo
ART DIRECTOR Jason Puffe
DESIGNER Jason Puffe
ILLUSTRATOR Jason Puffe

5 **DESIGN FIRM** Curtis Marketing Group,
St. Joseph, MN
CLIENT Minnesota Academy of Cosmetic Dentistry
PROJECT Logo
ART DIRECTOR Jason Puffe
DESIGNER Jason Puffe

6 **DESIGN FIRM** Design Central, Inc.,
Silver Spring, MD
CLIENT C.A.S.E.
PROJECT Lifelines for Kids
ART DIRECTOR J. Michael Chapman
DESIGNER J. Michael Chapman

7 **DESIGN FIRM** Design Central, Inc.,
Silver Spring, MD
CLIENT Cancer Research Foundation of America
PROJECT Celebremos La Vida
ART DIRECTOR Vicki Miller
DESIGNER Vicki Miller

8 **DESIGN FIRM** designTHIS!, Napa, CA
CLIENT vanderToolen Associates
PROJECT Logo
ART DIRECTOR Kim Shaeffer

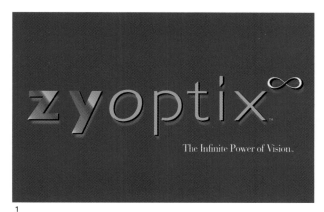

1

2

5

3

6

4

7

8

1 **DESIGN FIRM** DuPuis, Woodland Hills, CA
CLIENT Bausch & Lomb
PROJECT Zyoptix Brandmark
ART DIRECTOR Bill Corridori
DESIGNERS Bill Corridori, Jack Halpern
ILLUSTRATOR John Silva

2 **DESIGN FIRM** E3 Design Group, Elgin, IL
CLIENT Newell Office Products
PROJECT Locker Zone Logo
ART DIRECTOR Eric Engelby
DESIGNER Eric Engelby
ILLUSTRATOR Keith Handley

3 **DESIGN FIRM** Eagleye Creative, Littleton, CO
CLIENT The Rodeo Group
PROJECT Rodeo Icons
ART DIRECTOR Tom Pounders
DESIGNER Steve Schader
ILLUSTRATOR Steve Schader

4 **DESIGN FIRM** EC Design, Hackettstown, NJ
CLIENT Coldwell Banker Commercial
PROJECT 2001 Winter Conference Logo
ART DIRECTORS Elaine Coccaro, Kristin Levitskie
DESIGNER Kristin Levitskie

5 **DESIGN FIRM** G2, New York, NY
CLIENT Topps
PROJECT 50th Anniversary Logo
CREATIVE DIRECTOR Peter Lord
DESIGNER Danniles Konopka

6 **DESIGN FIRM** Geist Creative, Frisco, TX
CLIENT Miklis Printing
PROJECT Journey of Faith Logo
ART DIRECTOR Ben Geist
DESIGNER Ben Geist
ILLUSTRATOR Ben Geist

7 **DESIGN FIRM** Generator Studios,
West Chester, PA
PROJECT Logo
ART DIRECTOR Rich Hunsinger
DESIGNER Rich Hunsinger
ILLUSTRATOR Rich Hunsinger

8 **DESIGN FIRM** Glick Design, Kahului, HI
CLIENT Hyatt Regency Maui
PROJECT Grotto Bar Logo
ART DIRECTOR Robert Glick
DESIGNER Robert Glick
ILLUSTRATOR Jon Graham

1

4

5

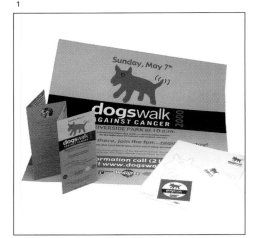

2

6

3

7

8

1 **DESIGN FIRM** Gumption Design, New York, NY
CLIENT American Cancer Society Eastern Division
PROJECT Kick Butt Teen Challenge Logo
ART DIRECTOR Evelyn Lontok
DESIGNER Evelyn Lontok

2 **DESIGN FIRM** Gumption Design, New York, NY
CLIENT American Cancer Society, Eastern Division
PROJECT Dogswalk 2000 Event Identity
CREATIVE DIRECTOR Evelyn Lontok
DESIGNER Nelson Wong

3 **DESIGN FIRM** HardBall Sports, Jacksonville, FL
CLIENT Mandalay Sports & Entertainment
PROJECT Shreveport Swamp Dragons Team Logo
ART DIRECTOR Michael O'Connell
DESIGNER John Massé
ILLUSTRATOR Michael O'Connell

4 **DESIGN FIRM** Hornall Anderson Design Works, Inc.,
Seattle, WA
CLIENT Twelve Horses
PROJECT Logo
ART DIRECTOR Jack Anderson
DESIGNERS Jack Anderson, Mary Chin Hutchison,
Lisa Cerveny, Don Stayner

5 **DESIGN FIRM** Houston Design, Norcross, GA
CLIENT Logic House Computers
PROJECT Logo
ART DIRECTOR Adam Houston
DESIGNER Adam Houston

6 **DESIGN FIRM** Jacqueline Barrett Design Inc.,
Oceanport, NJ
CLIENT Merck & Co., Inc.
PROJECT The International Twin Hair Challenge
DESIGNER Jacqueline Barrett

7 **DESIGN FIRM** Jones Design Group, Atlanta, GA
CLIENT Cereus Technologies
PROJECT Logo
ART DIRECTOR Vicky Jones
DESIGNERS Vicky Jones, Ann Vitek

8 **DESIGN FIRM** Kelley Communications Group,
Dublin, OH
CLIENT Rod's Western Palace
PROJECT 25th Anniversary Logo
ART DIRECTOR Kevin Ronnebaum
DESIGNER Jamie Havens
ILLUSTRATOR Mario Noche

1

7

8

3

5

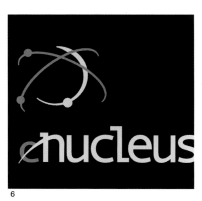

6

1 **DESIGN FIRM** Kircher, Washington, DC
CLIENT SkyRocketer
PROJECT Logo
ART DIRECTOR Bruce E. Morgan
DESIGNER Bruce E. Morgan

2 **DESIGN FIRM** Kym Abrams Design Inc., Chicago, IL
CLIENT Mike Walker Photography
PROJECT Logo
ART DIRECTOR Kym Abrams
DESIGNER Ryan Pikkel

3 **DESIGN FIRM** L.C. Williams & Associates, Chicago, IL
CLIENT AISA Technologies Inc.
PROJECT Logo
ART DIRECTOR Cynthia Calvert
DESIGNER Cynthia Calvert

4 **DESIGN FIRM** Lesniewicz Associates, Toledo, OH
CLIENT Lawrence Schmakel DDS
PROJECT Logo
ART DIRECTOR Terry Lesniewicz
DESIGNER Les Adams

5 **DESIGN FIRM** Mark Selfe Design, Emeryville, CA
CLIENT newmoon.com
PROJECT Logo
ART DIRECTOR Mark Selfe
DESIGNER Mark Selfe

6 **DESIGN FIRM** Monaco/Viola Incorporated, Chicago, IL
CLIENT enucleus
PROJECT Identity
ART DIRECTOR Mark Monaco
DESIGNER John Havemann
ILLUSTRATOR John Havemann

7 **DESIGN FIRM** New York City Economic Development Corporation, New York, NY
PROJECT Digital NYC Logo
ART DIRECTOR Randi Press
DESIGNER Randi Press

8 **DESIGN FIRM** Orbit Integrated, Hockessin, DE
CLIENT The PQ Corporation
PROJECT Go Soak Yourself Logo
ART DIRECTOR Jack Harris
DESIGNER Jack Harris
ILLUSTRATOR Jack Harris

iridian™
technologies

1

PLAGIARISM

5

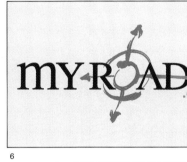

2

6

Balancing
Work & Life
at Philip Morris

3

xchange

7

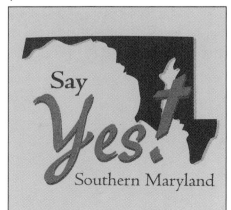

8

1 **DESIGN FIRM** Orbit Integrated, Hockessin, DE
CLIENT Iridian Technologies, Inc.
PROJECT Logo
ART DIRECTORS Bill Harris, Jack Harris
DESIGNER Mark Miller

2 **DESIGN FIRM** Philip Morris Management Corp.,
New York, NY
PROJECT 2001 Employee Survey
ART DIRECTOR Walter Kryshak
DESIGNER Walter Kryshak
ILLUSTRATOR Walter Kryshak

3 **DESIGN FIRM** Philip Morris Management Corp.,
New York, NY
PROJECT Balancing Work & Life
ART DIRECTOR Walter Kryshak
DESIGNER Walter Kryshak
ILLUSTRATOR Walter Kryshak

4 **DESIGN FIRM** Portfolio Center, Atlanta, GA
CLIENT Blue Dog Restaurant
PROJECT Logo
DESIGNER Sharla Helms

5 **DESIGN FIRM** Portfolio Center, Atlanta, GA
CLIENT Plagiarism
PROJECT Logo
DESIGNER Ameet Malhotra

6 **DESIGN FIRM** Primo Angeli Inc., San Francisco, CA
CLIENT MyRoad.com
PROJECT Logo
ART DIRECTOR Brian Lovell
DESIGNER Toby Sudduth

7 **DESIGN FIRM** RainCastle Communications, Inc.,
Newton, MA
CLIENT Xchange Applications
PROJECT Corporate Logo
ART DIRECTOR Jeannine Baldomero
DESIGNER Jeannine Baldomero
ILLUSTRATOR Jeannine Baldomero

8 **DESIGN FIRM** Sandra L. Edwards, Waldorf, MD
CLIENT Say Yes! Southern Maryland
PROJECT Logo
ART DIRECTOR Sandra L. Edwards
DESIGNER Sandra L. Edwards

1

6

LIBERTY LOGISTICS LLC

2

SAM

7

3

FilmFile DIRECT

4

5

1   **DESIGN FIRM** Shea, Minneapolis, MN
    CLIENT Dayton-Hudson's/Marshall Field's
    PROJECT Dayton's Mixed Greens-Tossed Fresh
    for You Salad Bar Logo
    ART DIRECTOR Holly Utech
    DESIGNER Holly Utech
    ILLUSTRATOR Jane Mjolness

2   **DESIGN FIRM** Stuart Bran Advertising, Allendale, NJ
    CLIENT Liberty Logistics LLC
    PROJECT Logo
    ART DIRECTOR Stuart Bran
    DESIGNER Stuart Bran

3   **DESIGN FIRM** Tribune Media Services, Chicago, IL
    CLIENT WebPoint
    PROJECT Logo
    DESIGNER Stephani Bode Kuehn

4   **DESIGN FIRM** Tribune Media Services, Chicago, IL
    CLIENT Film File Direct
    PROJECT Logo
    DESIGNER Lyle Anderson

5   **DESIGN FIRM** VLM Studios, Miami, FL
    CLIENT Homequest Realty
    PROJECT Logo
    ART DIRECTOR Vanessa Lam-Mendieta
    DESIGNER Vanessa Lam-Mendieta
    ILLUSTRATOR Vanessa Lam-Mendieta

6   **DESIGN FIRM** Walcoff Technologies, Fairfax, VA
    CLIENT DARPA Defense Sciences Office
    PROJECT Energy Harvesting Program Identity
    DESIGNER Vithaya Phongsavan

7   **DESIGN FIRM** Walcoff Technologies, Fairfax, VA
    CLIENT DARPA Defense Sciences Office
    PROJECT Structural Amorphous Metals Program Identity
    DESIGNER David Hoff

4

1

5

2

6

3

1 **DESIGN FIRM** What! Design, Allston, MA
CLIENT Single Parent Family Outreach
PROJECT Logo
ART DIRECTOR Damon Meibers
DESIGNER Brian Glogowski
ILLUSTRATOR Derek Aylward

2 **DESIGN FIRM** What! Design, Allston, MA
CLIENT North Shore Swimwear
PROJECT Aloha Swimwear Logo
ART DIRECTOR Damon Meibers
ILLUSTRATOR Derek Aylward

3 **DESIGN FIRM** Workbook & Company,
Los Angeles, CA
PROJECT Logo
ART DIRECTOR Zoe Korstvedt
DESIGNER Heather Scott

4 **DESIGN FIRM** Z Design, Olney, MD
CLIENT Creative Choices Pregnancy Center,
Outer Banks
PROJECT Logo
ART DIRECTOR Irene Zevgolis
DESIGNER Irene Zevgolis
ILLUSTRATOR Irene Zevgolis

5 **DESIGN FIRM** Zamboo, Marina Del Rey, CA
CLIENT MenuXpress
PROJECT Logo
ART DIRECTORS Becca Bootes, Andrew Werts
DESIGNER Jason Stillman

6 **DESIGN FIRM** Zermatt, Luling, LA
CLIENT Copeland's
PROJECT Internet Café Logo
ART DIRECTOR Stephany Geiling
DESIGNER Stephany Geiling
ILLUSTRATOR Matt Touchard

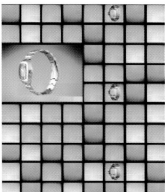

4

1

2

3

5

1 **DESIGN FIRM** Ariel Creative, Rockport, ME
CLIENT South Arm Campground
PROJECT Web Site
ART DIRECTOR Karan McReynolds
DESIGNER Ivan Castillo
PHOTOGRAPHER Dana Sigall

2 **DESIGN FIRM** be•design, San Rafael, CA
CLIENT Microsoft (Ultimate TV)
PROJECT Multimedia
ART DIRECTOR Will Burke
DESIGNERS Eric Read, Ron Bednar
ILLUSTRATOR Ron Bednar

3 **DESIGN FIRM** Canon U.S.A., Lake Success, NY
PROJECT System Software CDs
DESIGNER Steve Okon

4 **DESIGN FIRM** CBS Inc., Chestnut Ridge, NY
CLIENT 60 Minutes
PROJECT Broken Promises
ART DIRECTOR Roberto Corujo
DESIGNER Roberto Corujo
PHOTOGRAPHER Roberto Corujo
ILLUSTRATOR Roberto Corujo

5 **DESIGN FIRM** Courtney & Company, New York, NY
CLIENT IBB
PROJECT Monopoly Watch Presentation
ART DIRECTOR Mark Courtney
DESIGNER Christopher Quereau

1 **DESIGN FIRM** Creative Dynamics, Inc., Las Vegas, NV
PROJECT Holiday Card
ART DIRECTORS Eddie Roberts, Victor Rodriguez
DESIGNERS Casey Corcoran, Eddie Roberts, Victor Rodriguez,
Chris Smith, Mackenzie Walsh, Bob Zucco, Sally Hassler

2 **DESIGN FIRM** Design Headquarters, Jersey City, NJ
CLIENT Duda Penteado
PROJECT Riding with Joca
ART DIRECTOR Charles Flores
DESIGNER Charles Flores
PHOTOGRAPHER Charles Flores
ILLUSTRATOR Duda Penteado

3 **DESIGN FIRM** Fossil, Inc., Richardson, TX
PROJECT Big Tic
ART DIRECTOR Tim Hale
DESIGNERS Tim Hale, Stephen Zhang, John Vineyard
PHOTOGRAPHER Mark Underkofler
PRODUCER Mark Underkofler

4 **DESIGN FIRM** Fossil, Inc., Richardson, TX
PROJECT I Feel Good (Sunglasses)
ART DIRECTOR Tim Hale
DESIGNERS Tim Hale, David Eden
PHOTOGRAPHERS Paul Morgan, Stephen Zhang
PRODUCER Mark Underkofler

5 **DESIGN FIRM** Greenfield/Belser Ltd., Washington, DC
CLIENT Foley & Lardner
PROJECT Recruiting Web Site
ART DIRECTOR Burkey Belser
DESIGNERS Charlyne Fabi, John Bruns

3

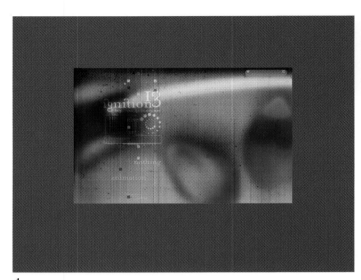

1

2

4

1 **DESIGN FIRM** ignition13 inc., Stamford, CT
PROJECT Interactive Exploration
DESIGNER ignition13 inc.

2 **DESIGN FIRM** Monaco/Viola Incorporated, Chicago, IL
CLIENT Georgia-Pacific
PROJECT Antitrust Seminar
ART DIRECTOR Bob Viola
DESIGNERS John Havemann, Rob Hicks

3 **DESIGN FIRM** Namaro, Inc., Rhinebeck, NY
CLIENT Henderson Brothers, Inc.
PROJECT Web Site
ART DIRECTOR Nadine Robbins
DESIGNERS Nadine Robbins, Molly Ahearn, Cindy Reifenberger

4 **DESIGN FIRM** Zamboo, Marina Del Rey, CA
CLIENT Futurekids
PROJECT SOLA Interactive CD
ART DIRECTORS Becca Bootes, Andrew Werts
DESIGNER Roy Dequina

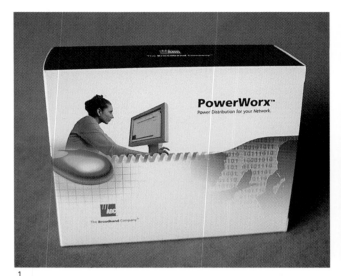

1

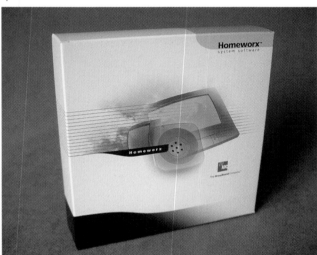

2

3

4

5

1 **DESIGN FIRM** ADC Creative Services Group, Eden Prairie, MN
   PROJECT PowerWorx Package
   ART DIRECTOR Mark Sexton
   DESIGNER Mark Sexton

2 **DESIGN FIRM** ADC Creative Services Group, Eden Prairie, MN
   PROJECT Homeworx Software Package
   ART DIRECTOR Mark Sexton
   DESIGNER Mark Sexton

3 **DESIGN FIRM** Axion Design Inc., San Anselmo, CA
   CLIENT Mission Foods
   PROJECT Tortilla Chips
   DESIGNER Ed Cristman

4 **DESIGN FIRM** Bailey Design Group, Plymouth Meeting, PA
   CLIENT William Grant & Sons
   PROJECT Dry Sack Gift Tin
   ART DIRECTOR Steve Perry
   DESIGNERS Wendy Slavish, Christian Williamson

5 **DESIGN FIRM** Bailey Design Group, Plymouth Meeting, PA
   CLIENT William Grant & Sons
   PROJECT Licor 43 Gift Box
   ART DIRECTOR Steve Perry
   DESIGNER Kelly Beh

1

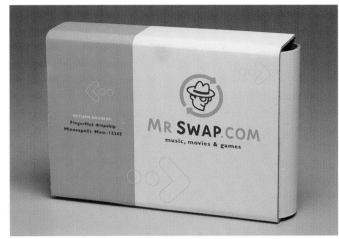

3

2

4

5

1 **DESIGN FIRM** Bailey Design Group, Plymouth Meeting, PA
  CLIENT Goldenberg Candy Company
  PROJECT Peanut Chews
  ART DIRECTORS Dave Fiedler, Steve Perry
  DESIGNER Denise Bosler

2 **DESIGN FIRM** be•design, San Rafael, CA
  CLIENT Mr. Swap
  PROJECT Packaging
  ART DIRECTOR Will Burke
  DESIGNERS Eric Read, Yusuke Asaka, John Meeks
  ILLUSTRATOR Yusuke Asaka

3 **DESIGN FIRM** be•design, San Rafael, CA
  CLIENT Hewlett-Packard
  PROJECT Packaging
  ART DIRECTOR Will Burke
  DESIGNERS Eric Read, Angela Hildebrand
  PHOTOGRAPHER William McLeod

4 **DESIGN FIRM** be•design, San Rafael, CA
  CLIENT Frontier Natural Products
  PROJECT Packaging
  ART DIRECTOR Will Burke
  DESIGNERS Eric Read, Suzanne Hadden
  ILLUSTRATOR Will Nelson

5 **DESIGN FIRM** be•design, San Rafael, CA
  CLIENT Cost Plus World Markets
  PROJECT Packaging
  ART DIRECTOR Eric Read
  DESIGNERS Eric Read, Coralie Russo
  ILLUSTRATOR Coralie Russo

1

2

1 **DESIGN FIRM** BKD Design, Fountain Valley, CA
CLIENT Contessa Food Products
PROJECT Contessa Complete Meals
ART DIRECTOR Jeff Barton
DESIGNER Jeff Barton
PHOTOGRAPHER Dan Wolfe
ILLUSTRATORS T. Vasabhuti, Craig Peterson

2 **DESIGN FIRM** Bloomberg, Princeton, NJ
PROJECT Mailroom Kit
ART DIRECTOR Sandy O'Connor
DESIGNER Verda Baslom

3 **DESIGN FIRM** Brown & Company Design, Portsmouth, NH
CLIENT Pure Barnyard
PROJECT Organic Potting Soil
ART DIRECTOR David Markovsky
DESIGNERS Tricia Miller, David Markovsky

4 **DESIGN FIRM** Circle R Group Advertising, Ft. Worth, TX
CLIENT Radio Shack Corporation
PROJECT Audio Cassette Tapes
ART DIRECTOR Allan Gould, Jr.
DESIGNER Rudy Abila
PHOTOGRAPHER Carl Nutt
ILLUSTRATOR Rudy Abila

5 **DESIGN FIRM** Circle R Group Advertising, Ft. Worth, TX
CLIENT Radio Shack Corporation
PROJECT VHS-C Cassette Tapes
ART DIRECTOR Allan Gould, Jr.
DESIGNER Rudy Abila
PHOTOGRAPHER Carl Nutt
ILLUSTRATOR Rudy Abila

3

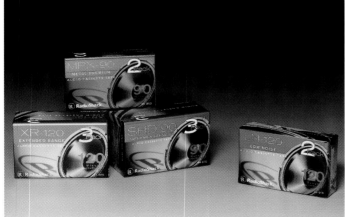

4

5

1

4

2

3

5

1 **DESIGN FIRM** Circle R Group Advertising, Ft. Worth, TX
CLIENT Radio Shack Corporation
PROJECT Grinch Toys
ART DIRECTOR Allan Gould, Jr.
DESIGNER Rudy Abila
PHOTOGRAPHER Roger Hein

2 **DESIGN FIRM** Cornerstone Design Associates, New York, NY
CLIENT Goodmark Foods
PROJECT Firecracker Brand Identity Redesign
ART DIRECTORS Keith Steimel, Sally Clarke
DESIGNER Martin Yeo
ILLUSTRATOR David O'Neil

3 **DESIGN FIRM** Design Guys, Minneapolis, MN
CLIENT Target Stores
PROJECT Henckels Knife Package
ART DIRECTOR Steven Sikora
DESIGNERS John Moes, Steven Sikora

4 **DESIGN FIRM** Design North, Inc., Racine, WI
CLIENT Agrilink
PROJECT Simply Grillin' Vegetable Package
DESIGNER Gwen Granzow
PHOTOGRAPHER Peter Hernandez, Studio 2
ILLUSTRATOR Eliza Lettering Design

5 **DESIGN FIRM** Deutsch Design Works, San Francisco, CA
CLIENT Anheuser-Busch Image Development
PROJECT 180 Energy Beverage
ART DIRECTORS Barry Deutsch, John Marota-AB Image Development
DESIGNER Gregg Perin

1

4

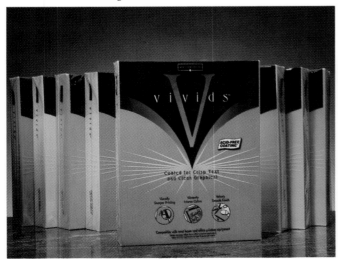

2

1 **DESIGN FIRM** Deutsch Design Works, San Francisco, CA
   CLIENT Safeway, Inc.
   PROJECT Select Great Escapes
   ART DIRECTOR Barry Deutsch
   DESIGNER Kate Green
   ILLUSTRATOR Bryan Haynes

2 **DESIGN FIRM** DiDonato Associates, Chicago, IL
   CLIENT Jim Beam Brands/Peak Wines International
   PROJECT Geyser Peak Block Collection
   ART DIRECTOR Nancy McGlothlin
   DESIGNER Nancy McGlothlin
   ILLUSTRATOR Nancy McGlothlin

3 **DESIGN FIRM** Directions Incorporated, Neenah, WI
   CLIENT Appleton Papers
   PROJECT Vivids Package
   ART DIRECTOR Kent Perrin
   DESIGN DIRECTOR Scott Mueller
   DESIGNER Paulette Brooks
   COPYWRITER ER Waskawic

4 **DESIGN FIRM** Directions Incorporated, Neenah, WI
   CLIENT Vande Walle's
   PROJECT Packaging
   ART DIRECTOR Kent Perrin
   DESIGN DIRECTOR Scott Mueller
   DESIGNER Paulette Brooks

5 **DESIGN FIRM** DuPuis, Woodland Hills, CA
   CLIENT Keebler
   PROJECT Sesame Street Snacks
   ART DIRECTOR Steven DuPuis
   DESIGNERS Bill Pierce, Al Nanakonpanom,
   Nobuko Komine, Jack Halpem, Steven DuPuis

3

5

1

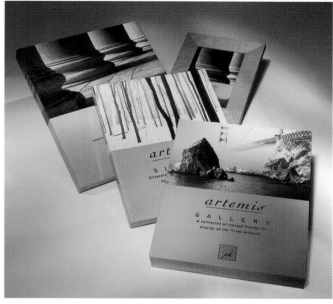

2

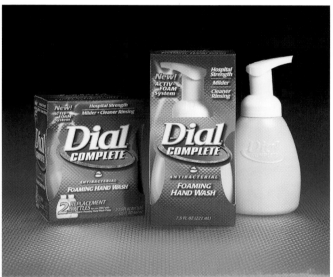

3

1 **DESIGN FIRM** EPOS, Inc., Santa Monica, CA
CLIENT Universal Music Latino
PROJECT Ignacio Peña-El Mundo Al Revés
ART DIRECTOR Gabrielle Raumberger
DESIGNER Matthew Neth
PHOTOGRAPHER Jill Kahn

2 **DESIGN FIRM** Federated Marketing Services, New York, NY
CLIENT Artemis
PROJECT Packaging for Artemis Frames
ART DIRECTOR Anthony Ranieri
DESIGNER David Lucas

3 **DESIGN FIRM** Fisher Design, Cincinnati, OH
CLIENT The Dial Corporation
PROJECT Dial Complete
ART DIRECTOR Peter Sexton
DESIGNER Lynne Chrapliwy

4 **DESIGN FIRM** Fisher Design, Cincinnati, OH
CLIENT The Scotts Company
PROJECT Max Guard
ART DIRECTOR Richard Deardorff
DESIGNER Richard Deardorff, Greg Goldsberry

5 **DESIGN FIRM** Franklin Design Group, Addison, TX
CLIENT Season Solé
PROJECT Tanning Lotion Tubes/Labels
ART DIRECTOR Wendy Hanson
DESIGNER Wendy Hanson
PHOTOGRAPHER John Knill

4

5

2

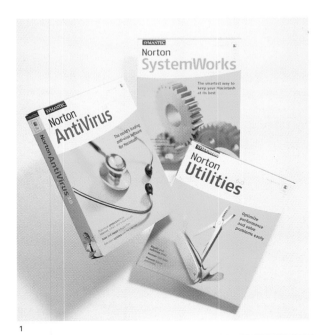

1

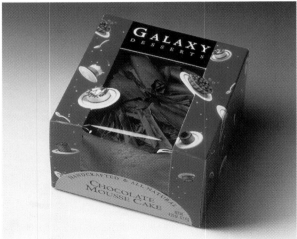

3

1 **DESIGN FIRM** frog design, Sunnyvale, CA
  CLIENT Symantec
  PROJECT Norton Consumer Packaging
  ART DIRECTOR Jean-François de Buren
  DESIGNERS Casey Potter, Gregory Hom, Roger Siu
  PHOTOGRAPHER Mark Cooper Photography

2 **DESIGN FIRM** Gammon Ragonesi Associates, New York, NY
  CLIENT Suiza Foods
  PROJECT PET Signature Collection Ice Cream
  ART DIRECTOR Mary Ragonesi
  DESIGNER Lael Porcelli
  PHOTOGRAPHER Manny Denner

3 **DESIGN FIRM** Gauger & Silva Associates, San Francisco, CA
  CLIENT Galaxy Desserts
  PROJECT Single Pack
  ART DIRECTORS Isabelle LaPorte, David Gauger
  DESIGNER Isabelle LaPorte
  ILLUSTRATOR Tom Reiss

4 **DESIGN FIRM** Gauger & Silva Associates, San Francisco, CA
  CLIENT Barbara's Bakery
  PROJECT Organic Crispy Wheats
  ART DIRECTORS Bob Ankers, David Gauger
  DESIGNER Bob Ankers
  PHOTOGRAPHER John Horvers

5 **DESIGN FIRM** Gunn Design, Boston, MA
  CLIENT 600 Lb. Gorillas
  PROJECT Packaging
  ART DIRECTOR Martha Heath
  DESIGNER Martha Heath
  ILLUSTRATOR William Duke

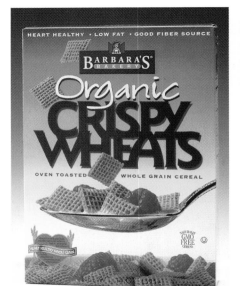

4

5

1

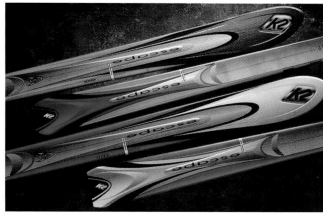

3

2

1 **DESIGN FIRM** Gunn Design, Boston, MA
CLIENT Avalon Beverage Co.
PROJECT Packaging
ART DIRECTOR Todd Damon
DESIGNERS Todd Damon, Jim Keeler

2 **DESIGN FIRM** Hasbro, Inc., East Longmeadow, MA
PROJECT Fun Funky Fingernails
ART DIRECTOR Deb Munson
DESIGNER ADG Graphic Design
PHOTOGRAPHER Jade Albert Studio
ILLUSTRATOR Laura Bolter

3 **DESIGN FIRM** Hornall Anderson Design Works, Inc., Seattle, WA
CLIENT K2 Corporation
PROJECT K2 Skis 2001 Series
ART DIRECTOR Jack Anderson
DESIGNERS Jack Anderson, Andrew Smith,
James Tee, Sonja Max, Mary Chin Hutchison

4 **DESIGN FIRM** Hughes Design Group, Norwalk, CT
CLIENT Reynolds Consumer Products
PROJECT Reynolds Creative Essentials Bright Ideas

5 **DESIGN FIRM** Hughes Design Group, Norwalk, CT
CLIENT Walnut Acres
PROJECT Organic Soup

6 **DESIGN FIRM** I.Q. Design Group, New York, NY
CLIENT Colgate Palmolive
PROJECT Ajax Laundry Detergent
ART DIRECTOR Leslie Tucker
DESIGNER Leslie Tucker

4

5

6

1

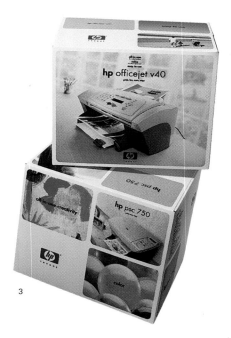

2

1 **DESIGN FIRM** Innovations Graphic Design Inc., Malvern, PA
CLIENT Home and Building Central.com
PROJECT Promotional CD
DESIGNER Lori Cooperstein

2 **DESIGN FIRM** Jensen Design Associates, Long Beach, CA
CLIENT Canon Computer Systems
PROJECT Brand Strategy Packaging/Collateral
ART DIRECTOR David Jensen
DESIGNER David Jensen

3 **DESIGN FIRM** Laura Coe Design Associates, San Diego, CA
CLIENT Hewlett-Packard Co.
PROJECT New 'Bi' Box Design
ART DIRECTOR Laura Coe Wright
DESIGNERS Tracy Castle, Jenny Goddard, Nancy Hearther
PHOTOGRAPHER Carl Vanderschuit

4 **DESIGN FIRM** Laura Coe Design Associates, San Diego, CA
CLIENT As We Change
PROJECT Personal Care Product Labels
ART DIRECTOR Laura Coe Wright
DESIGNERS Tracy Castle, Ryoichi Yotsumoto

5 **DESIGN FIRM** Logovations, N. Olmstead, OH
CLIENT Measurement Specialties, Inc.
PROJECT Scale Packaging Series
ART DIRECTOR Michael Lambert
DESIGNER Michael Lambert
PHOTOGRAPHERS Rick Zaidan, Zaidan Photography

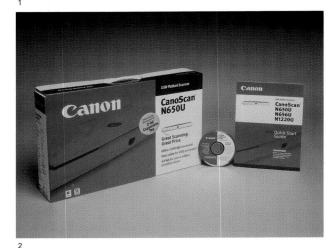

3

5

1

2

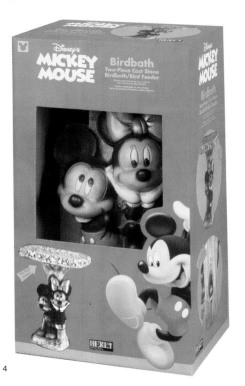

4

3

1 **DESIGN FIRM** Macey Noyes Associates, Wilton, CT
CLIENT Motorola Two-Way
PROJECT Motorola Talkabout Two-Way Radio

2 **DESIGN FIRM** MLR Design, Chicago, IL
CLIENT Kimberly-Clark
PROJECT Splash 'n Go!
DESIGNER Julie Winieski

3 **DESIGN FIRM** MLR Design, Chicago, IL
CLIENT Simply Orange Juice Company
PROJECT Simply Orange
DESIGNER Linda Voll
ILLUSTRATOR Lori Anzalone

4 **DESIGN FIRM** Para Designers Inc., Woodstock, IL
CLIENT Henri Studio Inc.
PROJECT Mickey Mouse Birdbath Package
ART DIRECTOR Eric Neumann
DESIGNER Mari Baskin

5 **DESIGN FIRM** Pepsi-Cola Company, Purchase, NY
PROJECT Slice Redesign
ART DIRECTOR Ron Udiskey
DESIGNER Ron Udiskey
PHOTOGRAPHER John Mierisch
ILLUSTRATOR T.P. Design

5

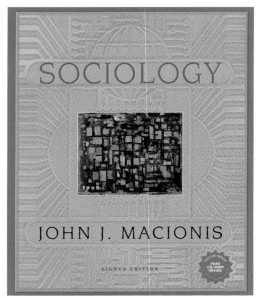

1 **DESIGN FIRM** PNY Technologies, Inc., Parsippany, NJ
  PROJECT Platinum CD-Rom Audio
  ART DIRECTOR Robert Palmer
  DESIGNER Robert Palmer

2 **DESIGN FIRM** Port Miolla Design, South Norwalk, CT
  CLIENT Kraft Foods
  PROJECT Capri Sun Big Pouch
  ART DIRECTOR Ralph Miolla
  DESIGNERS Jay Miolla, Ralph Miolla
  ILLUSTRATOR Peter Van Ryzin

3 **DESIGN FIRM** Prentice Hall, Higher Education, Upper Saddle River, NJ
  CLIENT Beth Gillett Mejia, Director of Marketing
  PROJECT Sociology, Eighth Edition
  ART DIRECTOR Robert Farrar-Wagner
  DESIGNER Robert Farrar-Wagner

4 **DESIGN FIRM** Primo Angeli Inc., San Francisco, CA
  CLIENT Aurora Foods
  PROJECT Chef's Choice Package Redesign
  ART DIRECTOR Rich Scheve
  DESIGNERS Chotima Buranabunpot, Kelson Mau,
  Vanessa Wyers
  PHOTOGRAPHER Jeff Kauck

5 **DESIGN FIRM** Primo Angeli Inc., San Francisco, CA
  CLIENT Imagine Foods
  PROJECT Soy Dream Package Redesign
  ART DIRECTORS Jennifer Bethke, Toby Sudduth
  DESIGNER Toby Sudduth
  PHOTOGRAPHER Michael Lamotte
  ILLUSTRATOR Rafael Lopez

1

2

4

3

5

1 **DESIGN FIRM** Primo Angeli Inc., San Francisco, CA
CLIENT Moosehead Breweries
PROJECT Packaging Redesign
ART DIRECTOR Jennifer Bethke
DESIGNER Oscar Mulder
PHOTOGRAPHER Philip Salaverry

2 **DESIGN FIRM** Primo Angeli Inc., San Francisco, CA
CLIENT Chupa Chups
PROJECT Package Design
ART DIRECTOR Lynn Ritts
DESIGNERS Toby Sudduth, Sean Baca

3 **DESIGN FIRM** Rock-Tenn Company, Norcross, GA
CLIENT Southern Food Specialties
PROJECT Bisquit Boxes
ART DIRECTOR Charles Hicks
DESIGNER Anne E. White

4 **DESIGN FIRM** S2 Design Group, New York, NY
CLIENT Brooklyn Bottling
PROJECT Nature's Own
ART DIRECTOR Eileen Strauss
DESIGNER Eileen Strauss
ILLUSTRATOR Lori Anzalone

5 **DESIGN FIRM** Shur Fine International, Inc., Northlake, IL
PROJECT Shurfine Redesign
ART DIRECTORS Wendy Sallak, Sandra Verdon
DESIGNERS Wendy Sallak, Sandra Verdon

1

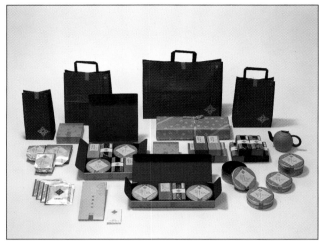

2

1 **DESIGN FIRM** SiD studios, Concord, OH
CLIENT Pierre's French Ice Cream Company
PROJECT Pierre's Authentic Frozen Custard
ART DIRECTOR Bill Sintic
DESIGNER Gina Bartlett
ILLUSTRATOR Pat Kilkenny

2 **DESIGN FIRM** SJI Associates Inc., New York, NY
CLIENT L'Epicier
PROJECT Jade Green Tea Garden Packaging
ART DIRECTOR GT Goto
DESIGNERS Rick Bacher, Karen Lemcke, Marie Coons

3 **DESIGN FIRM** Source/Inc., Chicago, IL
CLIENT Haggerty Enterprises
PROJECT Lava Brand Motion Lamp
ART DIRECTOR Adrienne Nole
DESIGNER Sabrina Chan
ILLUSTRATORS Doug Besser, Sabrina Chan

4 **DESIGN FIRM** Source/Inc., Chicago, IL
CLIENT The Clorox Co.
PROJECT Hidden Valley Dressings

5 **DESIGN FIRM** The Stanley Works, New Britain, CT
PROJECT MaxGrip Wrench
ART DIRECTOR Randy Richards
DESIGNER Daniel Deming

3

4

5

1

3

2

1 **DESIGN FIRM** The Stanley Works, New Britain, CT
PROJECT Goldblatt Display
ART DIRECTOR Randy Richards
DESIGNER Daren Eddy

2 **DESIGN FIRM** The Weber Group, Inc., Racine, WI
CLIENT SC Johnson & Son, Inc.
PROJECT Edge Active Care
ART DIRECTOR Anthony Weber
DESIGNERS Anthony Weber, Scott Schreiber

3 **DESIGN FIRM** The Weber Group, Inc., Racine, WI
CLIENT SC Johnson & Son, Inc.
PROJECT Skintimate Line of Products
ART DIRECTOR Anthony Weber
DESIGNERS David Sieveking, Scott Schreiber

4 **DESIGN FIRM** The Weber Group, Inc., Racine, WI
CLIENT SC Johnson & Son, Inc.
PROJECT Brite 1-Step Floor Shine Cleaner
ART DIRECTOR Anthony Weber
DESIGNERS Anthony Weber, Scott Schreiber

4

1 **DESIGN FIRM** Wallace Church, Inc., New York, NY
  CLIENT Taylor Made Inergel
  PROJECT Taylor Made Golf Pack
  ART DIRECTORS Stan Church, Nin Glaister
  DESIGNERS Nin Glaister, Paula Bunny
  STRATEGIST Cheryl Swanson

2 **DESIGN FIRM** Wallace Church, Inc., New York, NY
  CLIENT Snyder's of Hanover
  PROJECT Snyder's Redesign
  ART DIRECTORS Stan Church, Nin Glaister
  DESIGNERS John Bruno, Lawrence Haggerty

3 **DESIGN FIRM** Wallace Church, Inc., New York, NY
  CLIENT M&M Mars
  PROJECT Sour Skittles Candy
  ART DIRECTORS Stan Church, Nin Glaister
  DESIGNER John Bruno
  PHOTOGRAPHER John Lyons
  ILLUSTRATOR Lucian Toma

4 **DESIGN FIRM** William Fox Munroe, Inc., Shillington, PA
  CLIENT Hershey Foods Corporation
  PROJECT Twizzlers Twist-n-Fill
  ART DIRECTOR Thomas Newmaster
  DESIGNER Michael Amole

1

2

3

5

4

1 **DESIGN FIRM** Access TCA, Boston, MA
CLIENT NEC
PROJECT 3G P-O-P
ART DIRECTOR Finn Yonkers
DESIGNER Finn Yonkers
PHOTOGRAPHER Jamie Padgett
ILLUSTRATOR Finn Yonkers

2 **DESIGN FIRM** be•design, San Rafael, CA
CLIENT Audiobase
PROJECT Exhibits (Tradeshow Booth)
ART DIRECTOR Will Burke
DESIGNERS Carissa Guirao, Yusuke Asaka

3 **DESIGN FIRM** BOLT, Charlotte, NC
CLIENT G.H. Bass & Co.
PROJECT WSA Trade Show Exhibit
ART DIRECTOR Jamey Boiter
DESIGNER Duffy-Marie Ebel
PHOTOGRAPHERS Michael Harrison, David Sulwer

4 **DESIGN FIRM** Creative Alliance Marketing &
Communications, Southport, CT
CLIENT Pepsi Cola Company
PROJECT Pepsi Flavors Display Graphics
ART DIRECTOR Ann Lumpinski
DESIGNER Joe LaBash

5 **DESIGN FIRM** Cyberserv, Inc., Vienna, VA
PROJECT Customer-Facing Technologies Booth
ART DIRECTOR Patricia Poljak
DESIGNER Patricia Poljak

1

2

4

3

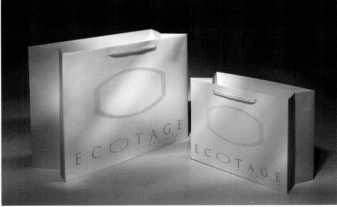

5

1 **DESIGN FIRM** DCI Marketing, Milwaukee, WI
CLIENT GMC
PROJECT Product Information Center Graphics
ART DIRECTOR Tom Bruckbauer
DESIGNER Tom Bruckbauer

2 **DESIGN FIRM** DCI Marketing, Milwaukee, WI
CLIENT Pontiac
PROJECT Aztek Launch Brandbook
ART DIRECTOR Tom Bruckbauer
DESIGNER Tom Bruckbauer

3 **DESIGN FIRM** Division Street Design, Westlake, OH
CLIENT Western Enterprises
PROJECT Western Medica Trade Show Graphic
DESIGNER Thia Peterson

4 **DESIGN FIRM** DVC Group, Morristown, NJ
CLIENT Labatt USA
PROJECT Tecate Music Program
ART DIRECTOR Marc Feil

5 **DESIGN FIRM** Federated Marketing Services, New York, NY
CLIENT Ecotage Salon & Spa
PROJECT Shopping Bags
ART DIRECTOR David Figueroa
DESIGNER David Figueroa

1

2

3

5

1 **DESIGN FIRM** Fossil, Inc., Richardson, TX
PROJECT Fossil Forever Kit
ART DIRECTOR Stephen Zhang
DESIGNER Dominique Pierron
PHOTOGRAPHER Dave McKormick
ILLUSTRATOR Ellen Tanner

2 **DESIGN FIRM** Gerard Hilferty and Associates, Inc., Athens, OH
CLIENT Orange County Regional History Center
PROJECT Citrus Exhibit
ART DIRECTOR Richard Woollacott
DESIGNER John Lauer

3 **DESIGN FIRM** Gerard Hilferty and Associates, Inc., Athens, OH
CLIENT Oklahoma Museum of Natural History
PROJECT Natural Wonders Gallery
ART DIRECTOR Mark Barnes
DESIGNER Greg Matty
PHOTOGRAPHER David Fox

4 **DESIGN FIRM** Hanson Carlson, Stamford, CT
CLIENT Winstar Communications
PROJECT e.center Multimedia Presentation & Technology Demonstration Exhibit
ART DIRECTORS Graham Hanson, Kendra Carlson
DESIGNERS Graham Hanson, Kendra Carlson, Yuji Yamazaki, Chris DiMaggio
PHOTOGRAPHER Scott McDonald

5 **DESIGN FIRM** Harman Consumer Group, Woodbury, NY
CLIENT Infinity Systems
PROJECT Intermezzo P-O-P
ART DIRECTOR Mike Keeley
DESIGNER Mike Keeley
PHOTOGRAPHER Josh McClure

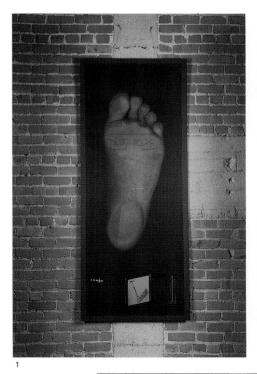

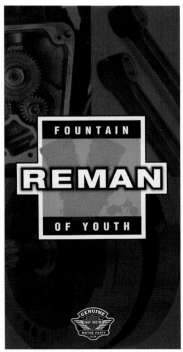

1

2

1 **DESIGN FIRM** Lunar Design, San Francisco, CA
CLIENT Xootr
PROJECT Exhibit Panels
DESIGNER Florence Bautista

2 **DESIGN FIRM** McCulloch Design Group, Waukesha, WI
CLIENT Harley-Davidson Motor Company
PROJECT Reman Tour Signs
ART DIRECTOR Ted Mayer
DESIGNER Ted Mayer
PHOTOGRAPHER Angie Rose, MDG Photography

3 **DESIGN FIRM** McMillan Group, Inc., Westport, CT
CLIENT Plant Equipment, Inc.
PROJECT Trade Show Exhibit
ART DIRECTOR Patty Schick
DESIGNER Charlie McMillan
PHOTOGRAPHER Jamie Padgett
ILLUSTRATOR Joe Toohey

4 **DESIGN FIRM** McMillan Group, Inc., Westport, CT
CLIENT Moss, Inc.
PROJECT Trade Show Exhibit
ART DIRECTOR Deb Curtis
DESIGNER Charlie McMillan
PHOTOGRAPHER Jamie Padgett

5 **DESIGN FIRM** Minx Design, Akron, OH
CLIENT Akron Symphony Orchestra
PROJECT Family Series Concerts
DESIGNER Cecilia M. Sveda

3

4

5

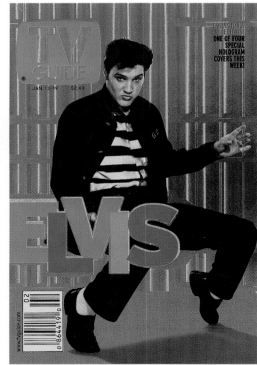

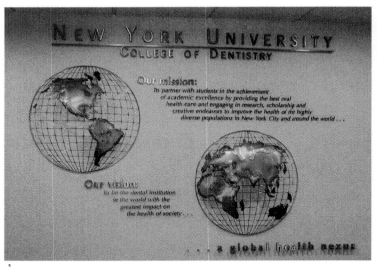

1 **DESIGN FIRM** NYU College of Dentistry, New York, NY
PROJECT Wall Display
ART DIRECTOR Marianne Jaycox
DESIGNER Marianne Jaycox

2 **DESIGN FIRM** Proma Technologies, Franklin, MA
CLIENT TV Guide
PROJECT Elvis Collector's Edition
DESIGNER International Holographic Paper

3 **DESIGN FIRM** Sayles Graphic Design, Des Moines, IA
CLIENT Mezzodi's Restaurant
PROJECT Signage
ART DIRECTOR John Sayles
DESIGNER John Sayles
PHOTOGRAPHER Bill Nellans
ILLUSTRATOR John Sayles

4 **DESIGN FIRM** Zermatt, Luling, LA
CLIENT Kajun Kettle Foods
PROJECT Tradeshow Backdrop
ART DIRECTOR Matt Touchard
DESIGNER Matt Touchard
ILLUSTRATOR Matt Touchard

1

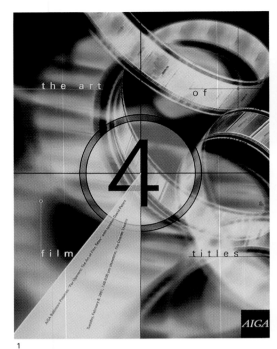

2

3

4

5

1 **DESIGN FIRM** 818 Studio Inc., Annapolis, MD
CLIENT AIGA
PROJECT Art of Film Titles Poster
DESIGNER Keith Johnston

2 **DESIGN FIRM** ADC Creative Services Group,
Eden Prairie, MN
PROJECT The ADC Way Poster
ART DIRECTOR Mark Sexton
DESIGNER Mark Sexton

3 **DESIGN FIRM** Berkeley Summer Sessions,
Berkeley, CA
PROJECT Poster
ART DIRECTOR Barbara A. Brown
DESIGNER David Lance Goines
ILLUSTRATOR David Lance Goines

4 **DESIGN FIRM** Brown & Company Design,
Portsmouth, NH
CLIENT Nature Conservancy
PROJECT Mount Agamenticus Poster
ART DIRECTOR David Markovsky
DESIGNER Claudia Kaerner
PHOTOGRAPHERS Harold Maude, Bill Silliker,
Charles Duncan

5 **DESIGN FIRM** Canon U.S.A., Lake Success, NY
PROJECT A.T.S.P. 2001
DESIGNER Steve Okon

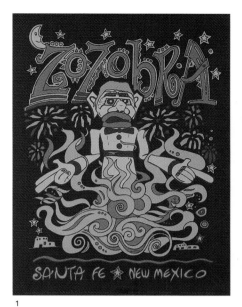

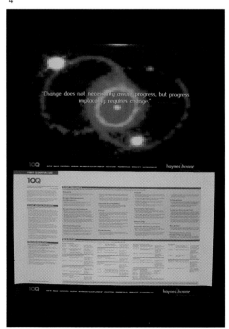

1 **DESIGN FIRM** Cisneros Design, Inc., Santa Fe, NM
CLIENT Santa Fe Downtown Kiwanis
PROJECT Zozobra Poster Series
ART DIRECTORS Eric Griego, Fred Cisneros
DESIGNER Eric Griego
ILLUSTRATOR William Rotsaert

2 **DESIGN FIRM** Designed Solutions, Kettering, OH
CLIENT Mondolux
PROJECT Money Shot Poster
DESIGNER Roger Owsley

3 **DESIGN FIRM** Getty Images, Seattle, WA
PROJECT Youth in Focus DoublExposure
ART DIRECTOR Michael Lindsay
DESIGNERS Jen Covington, Jack Middlebrooks
PHOTOGRAPHER McKeisha Ervin

4 **DESIGN FIRM** Gorman Richardson Architects, Hopkinton, MA
PROJECT Recruitment Poster
DESIGNER Doug Hill
PHOTOGRAPHER John Homer
ILLUSTRATOR Doug Hill

5 **DESIGN FIRM** Greenfield/Belser Ltd., Washington, DC
CLIENT Haynes and Boone
PROJECT 10Q Poster
ART DIRECTOR Burkey Belser
DESIGNER Tom Cameron

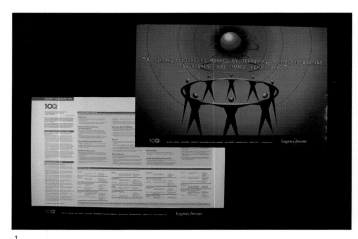

1

2

3

4

5

1 **DESIGN FIRM** Greenfield/Belser Ltd., Washington, DC
CLIENT Haynes and Boone
PROJECT 10Q Poster (People)
ART DIRECTOR Burkey Belser
DESIGNER Tom Cameron
COPYWRITER Lise Anne Schwartz

2 **DESIGN FIRM** Hardboiled, Atlanta, GA
CLIENT AIGA National
PROJECT Get Out the Vote Poster
DESIGNER Peter Borowski
ILLUSTRATOR Peter Borowski

3 **DESIGN FIRM** L.C. Williams & Associates, Chicago, IL
CLIENT Chicago Department of Transportation
PROJECT Poster
ART DIRECTOR Cynthia Calvert
DESIGNER Cynthia Calvert
PHOTOGRAPHER Gary Taber

4 **DESIGN FIRM** Litton Integrated Systems, Agoura Hills, CA
PROJECT Management Club Poster
ART DIRECTOR Linda Shalack
DESIGNER Linda Shalack
PHOTOGRAPHER Mike Marcus

5 **DESIGN FIRM** Litton Integrated Systems, Agoura Hills, CA
PROJECT Book Discussion Poster
ART DIRECTOR Linda Shalack
DESIGNER Linda Shalack
PHOTOGRAPHER Mike Marcus

1

2

3

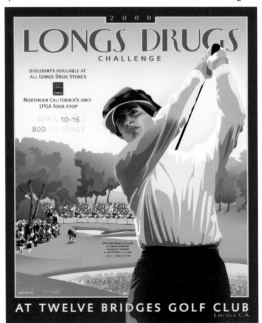

4

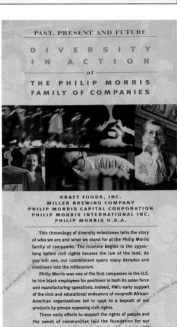

5

1 **DESIGN FIRM** Michael Fanizza Designs, Haslett, MI
CLIENT Michigan State University Department of Art
PROJECT Roy Carter Poster
ART DIRECTOR Michael Fanizza
DESIGNER Michael Fanizza

2 **DESIGN FIRM** Michael Fanizza Designs, Haslett, MI
CLIENT Michigan State University Department of Art
PROJECT Meighan Depke Poster
ART DIRECTOR Michael Fanizza
DESIGNER Michael Fanizza

3 **DESIGN FIRM** Northeastern University Publications,
Boston, MA
CLIENT Office of the Provost
PROJECT Artstuff Poster/Direct Mail
ART DIRECTOR Mary Beth McSwigan
DESIGNER Mary Beth McSwigan

4 **DESIGN FIRM** Page Design, Inc., Sacramento, CA
CLIENT Raycom Sports
PROJECT Longs Drugs Challenge Poster
ART DIRECTORS Paul Page, Chris Brown
DESIGNER Chris Brown
ILLUSTRATOR Kurt Kland

5 **DESIGN FIRM** Philip Morris Management Corp.,
New York, NY
PROJECT Diversity in Action
ART DIRECTOR Lorraine Chiarra
DESIGNER Walter Kryshak

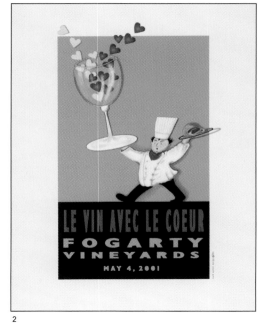

1

2

3

4

Born to Lose

5

1 **DESIGN FIRM** Sayles Graphic Design, Des Moines, IA
CLIENT Nebraska AIGA
PROJECT Art Farm
ART DIRECTOR John Sayles
DESIGNER John Sayles
ILLUSTRATOR John Sayles

2 **DESIGN FIRM** Suze Wilson Design Studio, Mill Valley, CA
CLIENT Stanford Vascular Research, Santa Cruz Mountain
Winegrowers Association
PROJECT Le Vin Avec Le Coeur
ART DIRECTOR Suze Wilson
DESIGNER Suze Wilson
ILLUSTRATOR Suze Wilson

3 **DESIGN FIRM** Ted Bertz Graphic Design, Inc., Middletown, CT
CLIENT Durham Fair
PROJECT Poster
ART DIRECTOR Ted Bertz
DESIGNER Dawn Droskoski
PHOTOGRAPHER Paul Horton
ILLUSTRATOR Dawn Droskoski

4 **DESIGN FIRM** Ted Bertz Graphic Design, Inc., Middletown, CT
CLIENT Middletown Garden Club
PROJECT Blossoms at Long Hill
ART DIRECTOR Ted Bertz
DESIGNER Dawn Droskoski
PHOTOGRAPHER Paul Horton

5 **DESIGN FIRM** The Humane Society of the United States,
Gaithersburg, MD
PROJECT Born to Lose
ART DIRECTOR Paula Jaworski
DESIGNER Paula Jaworski
PHOTOGRAPHER Steve Heaslip

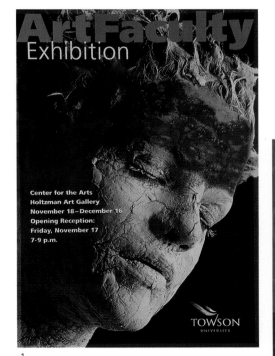

1

3

4

5

1 **DESIGN FIRM** Towson University, Towson, MD
CLIENT Art Faculty
PROJECT Poster
DESIGNER Kathy Malanowski

2 **DESIGN FIRM** Towson University, Towson, MD
CLIENT Holtzman Art Gallery
PROJECT Soup to Nuts
DESIGNER Kathy Malanowski

3 **DESIGN FIRM** VTS Travel Direct, Mahwah, NJ
CLIENT Corporate Accounts
PROJECT DirectLink
ART DIRECTOR Rebecca J. Lauth

4 **DESIGN FIRM** whiteSTARdesign, Bethlehem, PA
CLIENT Allentown Art Museum
PROJECT Nick Cave Poster
ART DIRECTOR Peter Stolvoort
DESIGNER Peter Stolvoort

5 **DESIGN FIRM** Zermatt, Luling, LA
CLIENT Cirque Du Soleil
PROJECT Invoke, Provoke, Evoke
ART DIRECTOR Matt Touchard
DESIGNER Matt Touchard
ILLUSTRATOR Matt Touchard

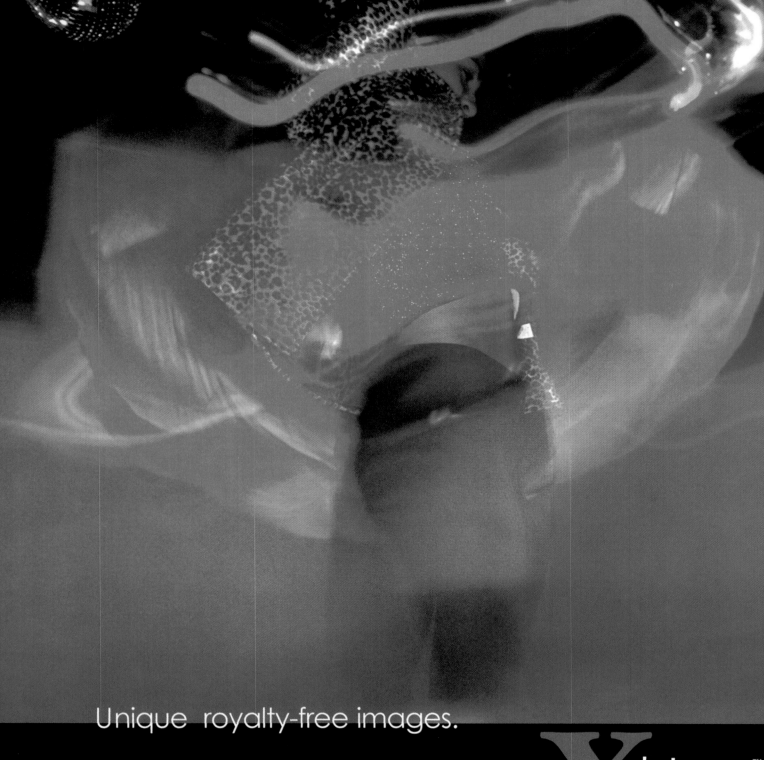

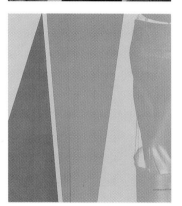

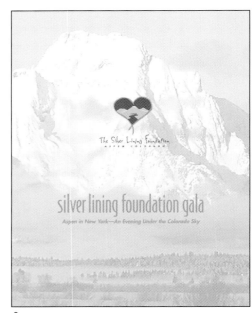

1

2

3

4

5

6

1 **DESIGN FIRM** Basilblue, Grimes, IA
CLIENT PRSA-Public Relations Society of America
PROJECT 2001 Prime Awards, Call for Entries
ART DIRECTOR Alicia Van Ausdall
DESIGNER Alicia Van Ausdall

2 **DESIGN FIRM** Bloomberg, Princeton, NJ
CLIENT The Silver Lining Foundation
PROJECT Gala Journal
ART DIRECTOR Sandy O'Connor
DESIGNER Ali Jeffery

3 **DESIGN FIRM** BOLT, Charlotte, NC
CLIENT Industrial Designers Society of America
PROJECT Design Gumbo
ART DIRECTOR Jamey Boiter
DESIGNERS Deanna Mancuso, Mark Thwaites,
Maureen Shaffron
PHOTOGRAPHER Stephanie Chesson

4 **DESIGN FIRM** Brown & Company Design,
Portsmouth, NH
CLIENT Pro Portsmouth
PROJECT First Night Fundraising Calendar
ART DIRECTOR David Markovsky
DESIGNERS Matt Talbot, David Markovsky

5 **DESIGN FIRM** Cisneros Design, Inc.,
Santa Fe, NM
CLIENT New Mexico Community Foundation
PROJECT Annual Campaign
ART DIRECTOR Brian Hurshman, Eric Griego
DESIGNER Eric Griego
PHOTOGRAPHER Don Usner

DESIGN FIRM Dennis Johnson Design,
Oakland, CA
CLIENT Children Now
PROJECT California Report Card 2000
ART DIRECTOR Dennis Johnson
DESIGNER Dennis Johnson
PHOTOGRAPHER Janet Delaney, Steve Fisch

1

2

3

4

5

6

1 **DESIGN FIRM** Dennis Johnson Design,
Oakland, CA
CLIENT Park Day School
PROJECT Secret Gardens of the East Bay 2001
ART DIRECTOR Dennis Johnson
DESIGNER Dennis Johnson
PHOTOGRAPHER Nicholas Pavloff

2 **DESIGN FIRM** Designed Solutions,
Kettering, OH
CLIENT Artemis Center
PROJECT Announcement
ART DIRECTOR Roxann Patrick
DESIGNER Designed Solutions Group

3 **DESIGN FIRM** DesigNan Graphics,
Burbank, IL
CLIENT Brookfield Zoo
PROJECT Employee Holiday Gift
DESIGNER Nan Brummerstedt

4 **DESIGN FIRM** First Light Design, Chicago, IL
CLIENT Franciscan Village
PROJECT Shooting Shamrock
ART DIRECTOR Sherry Trojniar Russo
DESIGNER Sherry Trojniar Russo
ILLUSTRATOR Sherry Trojniar Russo

5 **DESIGN FIRM** Hardboiled, Atlanta, GA
CLIENT AIGA Atlanta
PROJECT The AIGA Guide to Atlanta
DESIGNER Peter Borowski
PHOTOGRAPHERS Jerry Burns, Guy Welch

6 **DESIGN FIRM** Ison Design, San Francisco, CA
CLIENT New Leaf Services
PROJECT Bus Ad/Postcard
DESIGNER Annabelle Ison

1

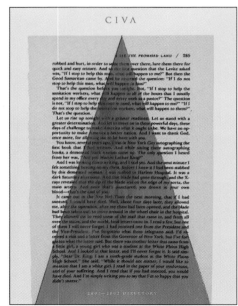

2

POND

Preserving Our Neighborhood Density

POND

3

zia ziprin

4

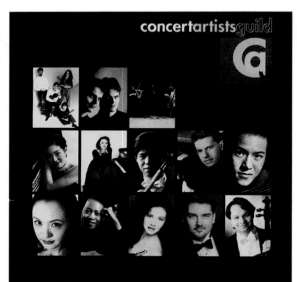

concertartistsguild

5

YOU SHOULD BE ASHAMED
TO WEAR FUR.

Be Fur-Free in the New Century.

1-800-HUMANE 1

6

1 **DESIGN FIRM** Keiler & Company, Farmington, CT
CLIENT U Mass Medical Center-Behavioral Sciences
PROJECT Quit Smoking Kit
ART DIRECTOR Aaron Dietz
DESIGNER Aaron Dietz

2 **DESIGN FIRM** Mission House Creative, Raleigh, NC
CLIENT CIVA (Christians in the Visual Arts)
PROJECT Directory
ART DIRECTOR Carol Roessner
DESIGNERS Carol Roessner, Roberta Lawrence

3 **DESIGN FIRM** Para Designers Inc., Woodstock, IL
CLIENT POND-Association of Homeowners
PROJECT Pro Bono Logo
ART DIRECTOR Eric Neumann
DESIGNER Mari Baskin

4 **DESIGN FIRM** Sichtwerk, Inc., Brooklyn, NY
CLIENT Zia Ziprin Fashion Design
PROJECT Magazine Spread
ART DIRECTOR Gabrielle Schies
DESIGNER Gabrielle Schies
PHOTOGRAPHER Wade Schields

5 **DESIGN FIRM** Siren Design, Inc., Tenafly, NJ
CLIENT Concert Artists Guild
PROJECT Roster 2000
ART DIRECTOR Irene Liberman
DESIGNER Irene Liberman

6 **DESIGN FIRM** The Humane Society of the
United States, Gaithersburg, MD
PROJECT You Should Be Ashamed to Wear Fur
(Bus Tail Light)
ART DIRECTOR Paula Jaworski
DESIGNER Paula Jaworski
PHOTOGRAPHER Walter Larrimore

1

2

3

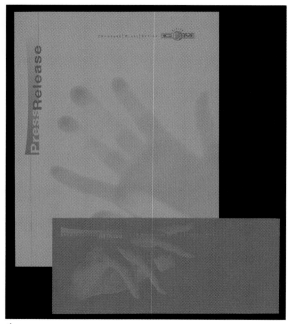

4

5

1 **DESIGN FIRM** 555 Design Fabrication Management, Chicago, IL
   PROJECT It's Time to Make Things Clear
   ART DIRECTOR Karen Herold
   DESIGNER Eamon Madigan

2 **DESIGN FIRM** Brandscope-Chicago, Chicago, IL
   CLIENT Radio-Flyer Inc.
   PROJECT 2001 Consumer Catalog
   ART DIRECTOR Bill Harper
   DESIGNERS Annette Ohlsen, Susan Hartline-Smith
   PHOTOGRAPHER Michael Roberts

3 **DESIGN FIRM** Courtney & Company, New York, NY
   CLIENT Michael Ryan Group
   PROJECT The Ritz-Carlton, Grand Cayman
   ART DIRECTOR Lynette Simmons
   DESIGNER Mark H. Courtney

4 **DESIGN FIRM** Crawford/Mikus Design, Inc., Atlanta, GA
   PROJECT Internal Press Release
   ART DIRECTOR Elizabeth Crawford
   DESIGNER Elizabeth Crawford
   PHOTOGRAPHER Scott Mikus

5 **DESIGN FIRM** Dart Design, Fairfield, CT
   CLIENT Tetley USA
   PROJECT Select Green Tea Sell Sheet
   DESIGNER Linda Anderson

1

2

3

4

5

1 **DESIGN FIRM** Directions Incorporated, Neenah, WI
CLIENT Gilbert Paper
PROJECT The Neutech Collection Paper Promo
ART DIRECTORS Chip Ryan, Chris Schudy, Gabe Quesada
CREATIVE DIRECTOR Lori Daun
COPYWRITER E.R. Waskawic

2 **DESIGN FIRM** Gammon Ragonesi Associates, New York, NY
CLIENT Anheuser Busch
PROJECT Budweiser/Michelob St. Pat's 2001
ART DIRECTOR Mary Ragonesi
DESIGNER Jill Schellhorn
PHOTOGRAPHER Greg Lord

3 **DESIGN FIRM** Gammon Ragonesi Associates, New York, NY
CLIENT Wasa Inc.
PROJECT Crispbread Promotion Brochure
ART DIRECTOR Mary Ragonesi
DESIGNERS Sarah Gurland, Alison Marston
PHOTOGRAPHER Greg Lord

4 **DESIGN FIRM** Gee & Chung Design, San Francisco, CA
CLIENT Applied Materials
PROJECT Tradeshow Bag
ART DIRECTORS Earl Gee, Fani Chung
DESIGNERS Earl Gee, Fani Chung

5 **DESIGN FIRM** Image Definition & Design, Inc., Chicago, IL
CLIENT Johnson Paper LP
PROJECT Paper PostCards & PaperView
ART DIRECTOR Patricia Kordas
DESIGNER Patricia Kordas
COPYWRITER Gregory L. Johnson

6 **DESIGN FIRM** JDC Design, Inc., New York, NY
CLIENT Pfizer Inc.
PROJECT Know Your Score Poster
ART DIRECTOR Jeff Conway
DESIGNER Paul Kiesche

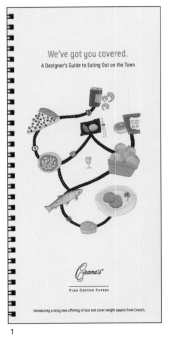

1

2

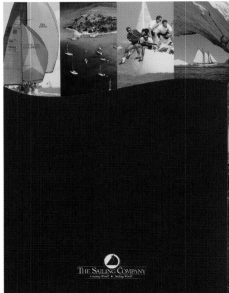

3

4

5

6

1 **DESIGN FIRM** Keiler & Company,
Farmington, CT
CLIENT Crane's
PROJECT We've Got You Covered
ART DIRECTOR Liz Dzilenski
DESIGNER Liz Dzilenski
ILLUSTRATOR Juliette Borda

2 **DESIGN FIRM** Keiler & Company,
Farmington, CT
CLIENT Crane's
PROJECT I.D.ology
ART DIRECTOR Aaron Dietz
DESIGNER Aaron Dietz
ILLUSTRATOR Paul Rand-Courtesy M. Rand,
Michael Schwab

3 **DESIGN FIRM** Miller Sports Group, New York, NY
CLIENT The Sailing Company
PROJECT Media Kit
ART DIRECTOR Cari Colclough
DESIGNER Kelly O'Connor

4 **DESIGN FIRM** Mosby/Harcourt Health Services,
St. Louis, MO
CLIENT Mosby
PROJECT GenRx Campaign
DESIGNER Tracy Dierkes

5 **DESIGN FIRM** Northeastern University Publications,
Boston, MA
CLIENT Center for the Arts
PROJECT Season Promotion
ART DIRECTOR Mary Beth McSwigan
DESIGNER Jane Winsor

6 **DESIGN FIRM** Orbit Integrated, Hockessin, DE
CLIENT The PQ Corporation
PROJECT Go Soak Yourself T-Shirts, Hats
ART DIRECTOR Jack Harris
DESIGNER Mark Miller

1

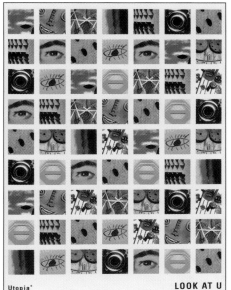

3

2

4

MORGAN STANLEY DEAN WITTER

• • •

ARE YOUR INVESTMENTS TAKING YOU
IN THE RIGHT DIRECTION?

• • •

5

THE PARK IMPERIAL

6

1 **DESIGN FIRM** Petertil Design Partners, Oak Park, IL
CLIENT Unisource/Neenah
PROJECT Neenah Classics Promo
ART DIRECTOR Julie Petertil
DESIGNER Julie Petertil

2 **DESIGN FIRM** Petertil Design Partners, Oak Park, IL
CLIENT Zebra Technologies Corp.
PROJECT Data Sheet Kit
ART DIRECTOR Kerry Petertil
DESIGNER Kerry Petertil
PHOTOGRAPHERS Benny Kende, Tom Balla

3 **DESIGN FIRM** Samata Mason, Dundee, IL
CLIENT Appleton Coated LLC
PROJECT Look at U Swatchbook
DESIGNER Samata Mason
PHOTOGRAPHER Sandro

4 **DESIGN FIRM** The Boston Globe, Boston, MA
PROJECT Parenting
ART DIRECTOR Lisa Sullo
DESIGNER Jessica Kurjakovic

5 **DESIGN FIRM** The Edelman Group, New York, NY
CLIENT Morgan Stanley Dean Witter
PROJECT Sales Promotion
ART DIRECTOR Terri Edelman
DESIGNERS Michelle Callot, Kazumi Goto

6 **DESIGN FIRM** Zinc, New York, NY
CLIENT Related Residential Development
PROJECT The Park Imperial-Sales Promotion Campaign
ART DIRECTOR Felicia Zekauskas
DESIGNERS Peter Maloney, Felicia Zeskauskas

sports imagery

model released

exceptional

concepts

images. life.

sport.

800 927 3638

request the new catalog today

concepts 2

1

2

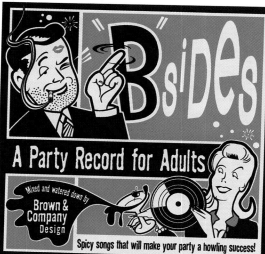

3

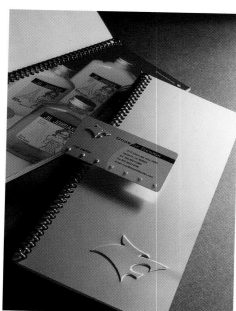

4

5

1 **DESIGN FIRM** Belyea, Seattle, WA
  PROJECT BrainStorm
  ART DIRECTOR Patricia Belyea
  DESIGNER Anne Dougherty
  ILLUSTRATOR Rep Art

2 **DESIGN FIRM** Berkeley Summer Sessions, Berkeley, CA
  PROJECT T-Shirt
  ART DIRECTOR Gary Penders
  DESIGNER Ran Bolton
  ILLUSTRATOR Ran Bolton

3 **DESIGN FIRM** Brown & Company Design, Portsmouth, NH
  PROJECT B-Sides
  ART DIRECTOR David Markovsky
  DESIGNERS Scott Buchanan, Matt Talbot
  ILLUSTRATORS Scott Buchanan, Matt Talbot

4 **DESIGN FIRM** Dart Design, Fairfield, CT
  PROJECT Bold Strategic Vision
  DESIGNER David Anderson

5 **DESIGN FIRM** Dogs of Design, Torrance, CA
  PROJECT Self Promotion
  ART DIRECTOR Max Parker
  DESIGNER Max Parker
  PHOTOGRAPHER Chet Carlbom

1

3

2

4

1 **DESIGN FIRM** DRC Advertising, Danbury, CT
PROJECT Elements
ART DIRECTOR Matthew Obstgarten

2 **DESIGN FIRM** Eagleye Creative, Littleton, CO
PROJECT Shirt Label
DESIGNER Steve Schader
ILLUSTRATOR Steve Schader

3 **DESIGN FIRM** Finished Art Inc., Atlanta, GA
PROJECT Merry Munchies
ART DIRECTORS Donna Johnston, Kannex Fung
DESIGNER Kannex Fung
ILLUSTRATOR Luis Fernandez

4 **DESIGN FIRM** Gayler/Graphix, Monroe, NY
PROJECT Sumo Santa
ART DIRECTOR A. Gayler
DESIGNER A. Gayler
ILLUSTRATOR A. Gayler

5 **DESIGN FIRM** Generator Studios,
West Chester, PA
PROJECT 310 Mayfield Avenue Series
ART DIRECTOR Rich Hunsinger
DESIGNER Rich Hunsinger
ILLUSTRATOR Rich Hunsinger

5

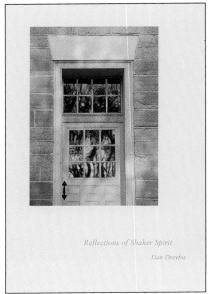

1

4

5

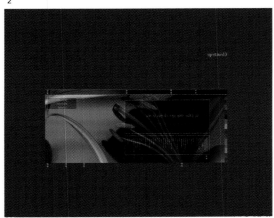

2

3

1 **DESIGN FIRM** Georgia Schmidt Design, Chesterfield, MO
CLIENT Dreyfus & Associates, Inc.
PROJECT Reflections of Shaker Spirit
ART DIRECTOR Georgia Schmidt
DESIGNER Georgia Schmidt
PHOTOGRAPHER Dan Dreyfus

2 **DESIGN FIRM** H, New Orleans, LA
CLIENT Corporate Realty
PROJECT Obituary Cocktail
ART DIRECTOR Winnie Hart
DESIGNER Gaby Tillero
PHOTOGRAPHER Kerri McCaffety's

3 **DESIGN FIRM** ignition13 inc., Stamford, CT
PROJECT Promotional Site
DESIGNER ignition13 inc.

4 **DESIGN FIRM** Inside Out Communications, Holliston, MA
PROJECT Self Promotion
ART DIRECTOR Matt Lynch
DESIGNER Matt Lynch
PHOTOGRAPHER Jim Kelly Photography

5 **DESIGN FIRM** Interbrand Hulefeld, Cincinnati, OH
PROJECT Teleidoscope/A Different Perspective
DESIGNER Jodi Sena

1

2

3

4

5

1 **DESIGN FIRM** Leo Bliok Advertising, Great Neck, NY
PROJECT Hard Times
ART DIRECTOR Leo Bliok
DESIGNER Leo Bliok
ILLUSTRATOR Leo Bliok

2 **DESIGN FIRM** Mackie Designs Inc., Woodinville, WA
PROJECT Wickedly Good Tee
DESIGNER Anna Welland
ILLUSTRATOR Anna Welland

3 **DESIGN FIRM** Michael Indresano Photography, Boston, MA
PROJECT Digital Capabilities Brochure
ART DIRECTOR Tom Laidlaw
DESIGNER Jonathan Grove
PHOTOGRAPHER Michael Indresano

4 **DESIGN FIRM** Port Miolla Design, South Norwalk, CT
PROJECT Self Promotion
ART DIRECTOR Ralph Miolla
DESIGNER Jeff Meyer
ILLUSTRATOR Jeff Meyer

5 **DESIGN FIRM** PrimeLook Inc., New York, NY
CLIENT Nickelodeon
PROJECT Baseball Cards
ART DIRECTOR PrimeLook Inc.
DESIGNER PrimeLook Inc.

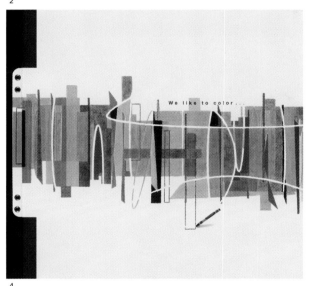

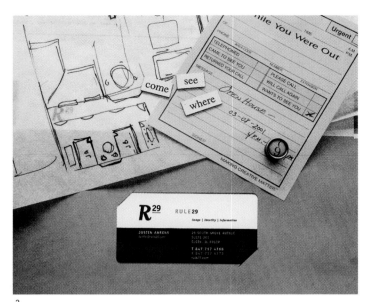

1

2

3

4

5

1 **DESIGN FIRM** Rector Communications, Inc., Philadelphia, PA
PROJECT Habitat for Humanity
ART DIRECTOR Cecile Hu
DESIGNER Dennis Beerley
COPYWRITER Don McCown

2 **DESIGN FIRM** Rule 29, Elgin, IL
PROJECT Opening Invitation
ART DIRECTORS Justin Ahrens, Jim Boborci
DESIGNERS Justin Ahrens, Jim Boborci
PHOTOGRAPHERS Justin Ahrens, Jim Boborci

3 **DESIGN FIRM** SJI Associates Inc., New York, NY
PROJECT Holiday Warm Up Kit
ART DIRECTOR Jill Vinitsky
DESIGNERS Rick Bacher, Karen Lemcke

4 **DESIGN FIRM** Skidmore Inc., Southfield, MI
PROJECT We Like to Color
ART DIRECTOR Mae Skidmore
DESIGNERS J. Pincus, T. Button, J. Latin, L. Hilpert, B. Nixon, P. Nothstein, C. Russell
PHOTOGRAPHER Jeff Hargis
ILLUSTRATORS B. Andrews, A. Bauer, G. Burgos, R. Burman, T. Button, L. Dodge, A. Foster, C. Gillies, R. Laubach, S. Magsig, D. O'Connell, B. Stolzenburg, R. Laslo

5 **DESIGN FIRM** The Edelman Group, New York, NY
PROJECT Self Promotion
ART DIRECTOR Terri Edelman
DESIGNERS Michelle Callot, Kazumi Goto

1

2

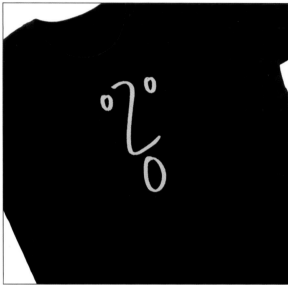

5

3

4

1 **DESIGN FIRM** The Indigo Group, Shelton, CT
PROJECT Starfish Story/Holiday Gift
ART DIRECTOR Dawn Tufano
DESIGNER Dawn Tufano
ILLUSTRATOR Dawn Tufano

2 **DESIGN FIRM** The Jones Payne Group, Inc., Boston, MA
CLIENT The Jones Payne Group
PROJECT Self Promotion
DESIGNERS Peter Raneri, Cheryl Gurvich

3 **DESIGN FIRM** Wallace Church, Inc., New York, NY
PROJECT 2000T
ART DIRECTORS Stan Church, Nin Glaister
DESIGNER Nin Glaister
ILLUSTRATOR Nin Glaister

4 **DESIGN FIRM** Wallace Church, Inc., New York, NY
PROJECT Thanksgiving Wine Turning of the Leaves
ART DIRECTORS Stan Church, Nin Glaister
DESIGNER Nin Glaister
PHOTOGRAPHER John Lyons

5 **DESIGN FIRM** ZGraphics, Ltd., East Dundee, IL
PROJECT New Identity Announcement
ART DIRECTORS Joe Zeller, LouAnn Zeller
DESIGNERS Renee Clark, Joel Davies

FIRMS REPRESENTED

INDEX TO ADVERTISERS